Pathway to Promise

DAVID ALEGE AKHAMIE, J.D.

Pathway to Promise

Copyright © 2018 by David Akhamie

ISBN 978-0-692-12258-7

All rights reserved. This book or any portion thereof may not be reproduced or used in any manner whatsoever without the express written permission of the publisher except for the use of brief quotations in a book review.

Editing by Jenny Margotta
Book design by StoriesTotellBooks.com

Contents

Foreword	i
Introduction	iv
Part I Etsa Kor "Those with the Split Teeth"	**1**
1. My Roots	2
2. The Biafra War	45
3. St. Peters Central Primary School	67
4. Caning, Discipline, and Lessons	75
5. Afe ("Family")	91
6. Mama, "The Humble One from Okpella"	105
7. The Changing Culture	121
Part II Iye Khee	**127**
8. The Enduring Codes	128
9. The Village Pride	133
10. Adolescence and Growing Pains	148
11. The Ventures of My Fathers	158
12. Our Lady of Fatima Boys College	165
13. Changing Times of Ye Khee People	175
14. The First Encounter	183
15. Enlightenment	189
16. The Enterprise Called Allah Dey!	196
17. Departure to the City	203
Part III Nigerian Man	**215**
18. Nigerian Man	216
19. Trip to Eko, Lagos	222
20. The Welcoming Place	230
21. Beyond the Ripples of Desert Storm	241
22. My Diaspora	246

Acknowledgements

There are people that I want to mention for their immeasurable help, support and encouragement:

My family of AKHAMIE as my circle of promise; Peter "the Rock" Agbaso Akhamie for his research, patience and support from the beginning through to the end, and Camellia Akhamie Kies.

Ava Williams; William Michael-Adikhai; Adamu S. Braimah; Evaristus Oshionebo; Evaristus Oshiokpekhai; Tijani Abu; Karen Ballard, Karen Dorse; Denice Seemiller; Emike Oyemade; Nigel Jason; Marcia Taylor; Foday Mansaray (my friend/brother with the United Nations – who tirelessly urged me to tell my story to help the youth of Africa) and the staff of Stories to Tell.

Foreword

A discussion of Nigerian literature often evokes memories of Chinua Achebe's epic novel, *Things Fall Apart*. It is evident that many readers became aware of the great Achebe of Nigeria during their college or university studies because *Things Fall Apart* was—and still is—a part of school curriculum in many parts of the world. Regrettably, however, many people outside Africa are not exposed to African literature, in part because of the vast global entertainment and electronic media which offer easy access to other forms of entertainment. In his book *Pathway to Promise*, David Akhamie attempts to rekindle and re-awaken a reading culture by espousing in amazingly accessible language.

Pathway to Promise is a narrative that will certainly enrich African folklore. It captures how Nigerian children were exposed to oral literature at a young age, which progressed into reading Achebe's books during high school. The author does so primarily by using his own life experiences, beginning with his humble upbringing in the little village of Afowa, Edo State, Nigeria. Because the author and his fellow Nigerian students could not afford to purchase books, they created a book-sharing platform whereby leisure reading became a communal experience, from one reader to another and from one village to another. Such networking encouraged young people in the villages to exchange knowledge and ideas in much the same manner as today's youth share chats, music, pictures, videos, "tweets", or what have you over the Internet.

I am fortunate to have witnessed some of the life-changing experiences captured so eloquently by the author in this book, because I was born and raised in the same Nigerian village.

In *Pathway to Promise*, the author portrays societies from the simple perspective of a village boy who, perhaps, saw things from a futuristic stance and beyond his years. The author reflects on the influence of living in the United States and being the last child of a large, polygamous family of four wives. In a childlike, inquisitive posture, the author draws from his mother's experiences as the youngest and last of his father's four wives. The author's childhood innocence is portrayed in simple prose everyone understands. The author flourishes in portraying various aspects of Nigerian societal norms prior to the Biafra War, from the village and town and onward into the tremendous forces of change that have swept through the nation since the war ended. Born in the '60s, prior to the Biafra war, the author provides a vivid account of the impact of the war on society and as the Nigerian cultures underwent change due to the tremendous influx of Western and other foreign ways.

The narrative touches on the author's departure from the village to seek greener pastures in the big cities of Benin City and Lagos, from where he travelled to the U.S. in quest of a university education. Upon his graduation from university, the author joined the U.S. Army and was soon deployed to the Middle East during the Gulf War. While on combat duties in the Gulf War in 1991, the author's beloved mother, Celina Amina Akhamie, passed away. The painful loss engendered in the author the desire to write *Pathway to Promise*, and his mother provides the inspiration for this book. This book also exposes the significant role played by the author's father while he was growing up in the village, including his pioneering feats as an enterprising entrepreneur.

The stories in *Pathway to Promise* are inspiring, funny, and at times emotional. Through insights from his career in professional law enforcement and public service with the U.S. Department of Homeland Security, the author has acquired unique storytelling abilities that will certainly inspire and motivate everyone, be they students, parents, or those who enjoy leisure reading about life's up and downs.

—Dr. Evaristus Oshionebo, Ph.D.
Associate Professor of Law
University of Calgary, Alberta, Canada

Introduction

I was born in a time of tremendous change and grew up in a village when people made fire for cooking by striking two rocks together. Once the wood was burning, the person who was able to start the fire would share the burning charcoal with neighbors. It was taken from one place to another, from the farm to the village, where it was used to start fires in kitchen fireplaces and for cooking meals. At night the older folks were kept warm by the slow-burning firewood. In the mornings they would borrow from the charcoal still burning through the night, and the circle of sharing would continue. There was no electric power in any of the villages.

About the same time that I became aware of the practice of sharing fires, I witnessed the electric generators that supplied electricity for the missionary quarters at night. They were the only electric lights throughout the whole of the Uzairue clan. The villages went dark at night, with the occasional bright spot from a kerosene lamp.

My life story began in the village of Afowa in Nigeria, and at that time, the majority of houses were built with mud and clay. The few wealthy families had corrugated zinc roofs on their homes, and the village collected money to send their smart students to the universities in faraway places. I attended elementary school in my village. It was not to my liking, but I continued to stay at home for the five years of secondary school, which was located in the neighboring town of Auchi.

One of the biggest societal changes during those years was the untenable political structure, like the wild fires that ignited during the upheavals of the Biafra War. After the war, there was great wealth from the oil boom, the experience of tremendous growth, and the boundless changes in our way of life, from rural subsistence farming to total dependence on petroleum.

My life in the village looked bleak to the extent of disillusionment after I completed high school. It was because of my awakening to reality that I vowed to make the best effort to take hold of my life. I relocated to the city to seek better opportunities, but a quick turn of events propelled me in another direction, and I ended up in the United States in 1981. Although I was in the United States, my heart remained close to the homey village of Afowa. It seemed like the missing part of an incomplete project, the persisting notion one faces to return and finish what one has started.

I did not consider that I was going to write a book, since my family history had always been passed by word of mouth. But I knew that the things I was told as a child were fading away quickly with the generations. The idea of putting the stories down in writing came from dreams of my mother. One of those dreams was the vivid reflection that began on a bright, sunny afternoon as I walked down to the village stream. The stream—called the Ugholomi—never dried up, even during the dry seasons under the tropical sun. It provided our potable water; it was always there, and it served as the multi-purpose venue like a marketplace where everyone went to get water, wash, ferment or clean the native foods, or as a casual meeting place. The women left their efor—a special delicacy of cassava—there to ferment. The washman went to the stream to wash clothes. As such, the Ugholomi was the center of life in the village; it sustained the people when other sources of water dried up during the dry seasons.

In another dream I was talking with my sister Aneke Cecilia about the marriage of her daughter. It had been proposed that the daughter marry Fidelis Ogbhemhe. In real life, however, Fidelis could not marry my niece; they were cousins. Weird also in my subconscious was the fact that Fidelis had died several years previously—in the 1980s—in a motor accident. Such things only happen in dreams.

"The proposed marriage is a good thing. Fidelis is a nice man who would take care of his wife, although he has a few personal problems." I said out loud to my sister as a token of encouragement.

The conversation switched to my first niece, Cordelia Idodo. She was Cecilia's daughter and my mother's first grandchild. My suggestion was that Cordelia should allow her daughter—the great-grandchild of my mother—to come to our house at Afowa where she would interact with other children.

"Rather than being kept away from the house, I think it would be a better home environment for the young girl." I said.

Aneke Cecilia faded from the scene as I walked down hill and over to the exact place where fresh spring water flows from underground. I was close to an area where the villagers fetched water. It overlooked the entire watercourse and faced the opposite side, the side leading towards Afowa. The junction is where the peoples from Afowa and Afashio villages meet and walk upstream to fetch the clean water.

There was a family—a mother and two boys—who were cleaning household belongings which were folded up as they prepared to depart uphill towards Afowa. Still a bright-sunshine day, one of the boys and the mother were all packed and waiting for the other son. They were getting impatient as the younger boy lingered, wasting time. One *oyibo*—a white guy—helped in getting the slower boy to finish up and be done. With a grudging smile, the boy's expression showed he had known all along what he had to do but had only pretended not to know. Finally, the family walked away.

The oyibo also faded from the scene, and I was alone with my mother in the deserted place. I stared, as my mother had died in 1990; so I was reassured it was all a dream. I walked up closely to her. It did not seem strange for me at first to be alone with her. I was a mature young man and seemed comforted to be with my mother, who had placed a pail of water on her head.

Mama said, "Fetch water." Although she already had a pail that she was taking home, she asked me to fetch more. "The water you collect will be used to bless the *ivwia,* the children."

My thinking was that a message was emerging from Mother for me to pass on. But she said, "You have to say words of prayer," as I searched for a container to collect some water for her.

I looked away and saw the plastic containers which I could use were buried halfway in the white sand. Then, in my dream, the scene suddenly changed seasons—from the moment of summer sunshine when I came down the stream to the tropical, raining season. It was during the raining season that those plastic containers were buried due the huge water flow. In the raining season, fewer people came to the stream.

Mother mentioned again in her soft but assertive voice, "Say the prayers!"

I began, "*Eda* (river) Ugholomi, I am here again, at this moment, and when I come to see you again, I will have aged …" or something of that nature. I repeated, "I am here … and I will come back again in another time. I promise."

As I said the words, I noticed that I had aged and was now showing a sprinkle of white-gray in my hair, a sneak-peek into my future life of middle age. I could sense Mother was not pleased with such invocations, as she turned to face me and said softly, "Say that prayer another way…" I responded in reserved confusion, so I noticed when the suggestion came, "Proclaim the prayers of blessing!"

I doubted still—without appearing to be conjuring diabolical entities of superstitious powers—whether I knew exactly what prayers

Mother wanted. However, I noticed that Mother was of a youthful age of about forty-five; she wore a lapa—that long piece of cloth the women tied snugly below the armpits, exposing upper shoulders, and that dropped to the knees. Meanwhile, the pail of water still remained balanced on her head, buffered by an *aeki* (head-roll).

She waited patiently, but we both knew we had to walk away from there. Before I could fetch the water, the day began turning from sunshine to shadow. Our attention was drawn to growing lights in the direction of the waterway about 100 feet away. I felt a connection with the light that suddenly appeared in the distance, but Mother wanted to face away from it, so I held onto her face to ensure she watched the lights. I said, "Do not be afraid, Mama."

Suddenly, the lights turned into a bright shape, then transformed into a halo, and I instantly invoked out loud, "Mama, it is the Virgin Mary!"

I recall another similar but unforgettable dream in the same place. Amazing flares which lit the entire forest placed the imagery in my mind of the entire area being electrified. This dream and others awakened something that revived those nostalgic childhood feelings of separation from my village, my adulthood, and the changes in my life

Tradition and reverence for ancestors were the way of life. However, Mother had converted to Christianity, and her faith had grown stronger when she gave her life to Jesus Christ. She vowed not to worship idols as gods. In the household, she was the youngest of the four wives, which made the choice of Christian teachings her own way of fulfilling her sense of faith. God preserved her life to see the answers to her prayers. She should have lived to an old age and been able travel around the world, but she died just before I asked her to come and stay with me in Germany.

The bitterness over Mama's death, coupled with dislike of the Gulf War, created a horrible experience that lingered with me for a long time. My thoughts and mind were appeased through those dreams, which showed me the way my mother lived her life. She believed that one should not hold onto the past but should live for the future.

At the time of the Gulf War, I did not know that my mother was critically ill. Letters took weeks, sometimes months, to reach Germany from Nigeria. When I was contacted through the International Red Cross, I had already been deployed from Germany and was in the Saudi desert. Mother's illness had been diagnosed in November 1990, but I could not accept the extent of her condition. I was terribly downcast but refused to accept the reality of the seriousness, internally confident she would be cured. I did not know that her breast cancer would not be cured.

I started to capture the peculiar dreams in writing because of the similarity of war experiences that were intermingled with the pain I knew my mother was enduring. I held a notion it was because of the affinity I held for my Mother, which was affirmed in conversations before she died. But I was convinced I needed to record the many stories of life with Mama, accounts of worldly experiences, interactions with soldiers, and more that involved many humbling moments. I documented these in my journals.

Through the experiences of my childhood, and reassurances from the dreams about my Mama, I have learned to accept that I was at the locus where I would have to write and pass on the stories of the silent voices we no longer hear. There comes a time in one's life at war, as in normal, everyday life, that many things happen, and individuals have differences about the exact same things; such is the purpose of life.

—David Alege Akhamie

David Akhamie

PART I

ETSA KOR

"THOSE WITH THE SPLIT TEETH"

Smiling because happiness was a virtue by tradition that spurred the filing of a split in the front teeth

Chapter 1

My Roots

Afowa is a small village known for its peace and tranquility, and everyone lived like they were related by blood. Everyone shared in the successes and hard times because an injury to one was an injury to all. There were the houses—huts, really—with thatched roofs, located behind the few modern houses with corrugated zinc-roofs that lined the single, main road. Footpaths branched from the main road like one was going into the wilderness. The source of information was through rumors spread from mouth to mouth. Life was shared through communal engagement; marriage was considered a ceremony of the entire village. The birth of a child was celebrated by all.

I was born in 1961. Nigeria had just attained her independence from Britain on October 1, 1960. Like the country's separation from Great Britain, there was anxiety over the future, which at that time was uncertain. Because of short life expectancies, primarily because of the high rate of infant mortality, there were no guarantees that one would live. The situation was alike for every child.

As soon as a woman married, she began to bear children. If not, she would be considered "bad luck" to the family. It was even worse if her children died at infancy. She could even be accused of witchcraft.

The child who survived to reach school age had beaten the odds, like one who went to war against evil forces and survived. Folks had to contend with ever-present traditions. Whether a nativist—such as the voodoo doctor—or a farmer, trader, Muslim, Christian, animist, etc., no one was expected to remain tied to their mother's apron strings for long. Every household must have offspring so there would be someone who would take care of the parents in their old age. My father, Akhamie Osigwe, I saw as a great man who had many children from many wives.

As the patriarch of a large family, his children took as their surname Akhamie, which is our father's first name.

I estimate that he was over sixty years old when I was born. He was about five feet ten inches tall and light "yellow" in complexion. Father had missing front teeth, which was customary for his age. He was a calm and quiet man who keenly listened to others and infrequently spoke, generally in a calm, firm voice. His eyes were sharp as if they were speaking for him, accompanied by intricate yet distinctive facial expressions. The years of catering to his large family had changed him for the better as a person. Everyone in the household often referred to him by the native names of Baba and Eramha (meaning Dad or Father).

Amina Celina Akhamie, my mother, the last of his wives, had children but also "bad luck," as some of her babies did not survive. The "good luck" was that I survived, although three were stillborn after me. Mama told stories of the sad experiences with infant mortality and her lifelong joy for the lives of her surviving children.

"I didn't give up. I tried to have more children," Mama told me. She believed that the more children, the better. Children represented a wealth of human resources and God's blessings.

"Three babies came after you. They did not survive." She would say, "I gave birth to eleven children, including a set of twins. Only five of you survived." Sometimes, she would answer my worrisome, inquisitive questions by saying, "I now live my life for you—my children. I want to survive so that I can see you grow up in this house!"

My parents Akhamie and Amina

I was concerned that I was the last child, but I conceded to Mama by accepting her explanation. Grudgingly, I said, "Mama, I am happy that I have my family and siblings—Philip, Peter, Cecilia, and Paul."

The idea of Afe, which means "family" in the tongue of Afemai, was highly cherished, as was the group and community we belonged to as one family. There were no registered records of birth, and many did not know their exact birth date. No one around me celebrated birthdays, since it was not part of our tradition. I did not celebrate birthdays then; of course, I didn't know my actual birth date, which was of less concern than my age group and mates. It could have been enjoyable or memorable for me to have birthdays, but it did not matter if I missed out on something.

Based on my estimation, Mama was in her late thirties when I was born. She had a youthful look, stood about five feet six inches tall, and was skinny. Mama had a dark, shining complexion and smooth round face. Her voice was distinctively soft, not shrill, and always had a soft polite tone. She had mostly lost the dialect and accent of

Okpella, where she was born, and had excellent command of our dialect of Uzairue. However, it was well known in the village that she was not native born, which gave her a certain sense of pride. Mama was a humble, conscientious woman, always looking for the best in every person and situation.

Mama was quite comfortable with her modest looks. She always dressed with the native lapa cloth fastened comfortably around the chest over the native buba, or blouse. Her hair was thick, full, and dark but was always cut short since she did not plait her hair. She explained, "I do not plait my hair because it makes my head hurt. A woman carries loads on her head. Only one desperate for beauty would plait her hair to go to the farm."

Mama was a natural, down-to-earth person. When she wasn't going to the farm, she would dress in the traditional lapa and buba and always wore the native head tie, especially for church and on market days. Her life was full and the village offered the ideal place to raise our family.

As the last of my father's children, there were certain privileges that I enjoyed. However, I often overplayed my hand when I acted out by crying because I wanted more. I cried at a howling intensity to get my way. Mama said, "A child would not cry blood from tears. You can stop when your mouth gets tired!" She stood firmly on her beliefs. "No one was going to have spoilt brat for a son." At the age of three, I was expected to join in the family activities; we walked everywhere on bare feet, from the village to the farm. No one wore shoes to walk around, and those who had flip-flops/slippers wore them only for special occasions. When I got tired of walking, Mama often ended up carrying me along the way, since I couldn't keep up. There was no younger sibling after me; I thought that Mama had to cater to my needs.

"Agbasovhelo, here, help me carry him," Mama called to Peter.

"Come on, get on my back," Peter said as he squatted to lift me up."Mama, he is a heavy boy now. Oh, he should be able to walk."

"Agbasovhelo! How do you expect him to walk up the hill?" Mama said, "You know how much I labored for you, um! Look at those deep gorges on the way. You expect him to crawl after I just bathed him? You think the child can walk by himself?"

"Mama, but ..." Peter said, but she was took the words right out of his mouth.

"Mama me for what? You are always smiling. Next time you will have to carry the pail of water on your head."

Peter Agbasovhelo is my older brother, and in between us there is Philip. Although he was far older than me and Philip, Peter had to help Mama with household chores since we did not have a young sister in our midst.

Mama called Peter Agbasovhelo, meaning "life is good for the eyes," and everyone seemed to like the name because of its positive redemption. We called him "Agbaso" or "life is good," which made Mama's scolding sound amusing, since one cannot rebuke and with the same breath call, "Life is good."

One of the women who admired Peter would caution Mama, "Amina, you leave Agbaso alone. He is a big boy now. He cannot be with you like a girl-child. Let him go with his mates."

From the distance one could see Agbaso was always beaming with cheerful smiles. He always smiled with his mouth wide open, displaying his sparkly white teeth as if he were enjoying every moment of the day—just like his native name Agbasovhelo, "life is good for the eye."

Peter was tall, skinny, and had a darker complexion which resembled Mama's skin tone. He had a quiet personality like our parents, a really caring personality and a distinguished character. His calm personality allowed him to be poised, and he would smile as he helped Mama look out for me and Philip.

Along the way Mama would strap me on her back with a lapa, supported with a hand-woven band called an oghia, and set off for the okhotohime (farm). She would carry a load balanced on her head, buffered by a rolled cloth called an eki (pronounced haykey). The practice of carrying loads on the head is the traditional African way for woman and children to transport goods. The fathers have a special bag resembling a rucksack strapped from the shoulder, as it was seen as an indignity for real men to balance heavy loads on their heads.

On trips from the farm, Mother would walk to a five-way junction, where one of the bush paths led to the stream called Ugholomi, located at the bottom of the valley, about a half mile from the main road. At the resting place, she would offload the pail-load of farm produce from her head and place it under the shade provided by the trees. The loads were usually placed in groups, family by family, as they arrived, before the peopled walked towards the stream. The loads left by the roadside—where they remained unattended under the shade—provided clues for passersby that someone had walked away towards the stream.

One was hardly ever alone, and almost like a synchronized clock, other women would join and the group would walk together. It was during these times that the conversations retraced old talks, the people's voices echoing away in the forest. It is meaningful between one, two or three friends in a group, but when others join in meaningful conservation, it becomes a challenge.

We would walk and meander to avoid shallow pits along the path. Slowly, direct sunlight was lost in the shade of the tall trees. We would be surrounded by the smell of damp vegetation, of fresh evergreen forests, and tall trees shading the stream. Even without rain, the shade presented the appearance of looming rainfall. A bath in the spring water provided relief from the heat and was always refreshing.

The women's area was sectioned off; they could wash or bath nude, although sometimes they wore their waist beads. The colorful beads, mostly black and sectioned with a few red beads, were the ornaments of beauty of the day. When the water was scooped with both hands folded, or with a calabash splashed on the body, sounds of audible chill signaled that cold was felt. To a child jumping into the cold water, it was just an exercise or another playtime.

I saw a happy boy who jumped with both feet into the water as the mother tried to get hold of him. "Come here! Don't waste my time. It is not playtime, wash yourself!" Okpo continued to pretend it was playtime; and the mother grabbed him by one hand and scrubbed his body with the other. "Come on, raise one leg. Now raise the other. No! Give me your right leg!" The exercise called bath was done within minutes.

I waited with demure patience until it was my turn to be washed. No excuse would save the day as the splashes of cold water landed on my forehead and body. The water would run down my face, creating a unique excitement as it reached my lips. The wash involved scrubbing my body with a sponge and black soap lather from head to toe. The lather would fall onto the water and quietly flow away as it landed.

At times the stream was less congested, and Mother would perform an act of teeth cleaning. A pinch of clean fine sand was collected from the sediment at the bottom and placed in the mouth. The index finger rubbed briskly from front to back teeth, back and forth, and the mixture was followed with clean water scooped with both palms and swished between the teeth before it was spat out. The slow-moving stream carried the liquid away. Although I resisted the idea, I quickly got used to it and enjoyed cleaning my teeth in the same manner. We did not have toothpaste or toothbrushes, only natural chewing sticks to be used as toothbrushes.

Upon my return several years after I moved away from the village, my sightseeing visit to Ugholomi brought back those memories. While at the stream, I scooped a handful of the pure sand, which I swished and twisted in my mouth with my index finger. Once the sand is spit out of the mouth, it leaves behind a sparkling feeling of fresh breath. I was glad to relive the experience but glad I did not have to disrobe for a wash.

The spectacle of our cold bath over, we had to walk up the hill, which was a challenge for the average three-year-old. Sometimes, Mother would carry me on her back up the hill to the Y junction. There were times when it got quite exhaustive to walk. I mastered clever schemes to get Mother to carry me on her back.

"Amina!" one of our feisty relatives called out to my mother. "You are spoiling that child by carrying him around."

I could sense the displeasure of the women. I really wished they would leave Mother alone and not to worry her with their gaffes so we could have peace and quiet until we arrived at the village. They did not relent, and I did not get my wish to be carried so that I could doze into a catnap.

My mother might resort to her own trickeries to get me to climb down and walk on my own. She would let loose with an outpouring of praises. *Adebidi Asamalli, Udala ubele, ogie neini, ogie luku luku.*" (David, like the king of Mali, shining in black. King surpassed the elephant; king honorable.)

Mama was referring to King David as "king of kings." In the Uzairue dialect, "ogie neini" means "the king of all," and it was one of her ultimate praises to boost my ego. She realized that sweet talk worked on me better than spanking. As the soothing of my ego took effect, I would climb down from Mother's back without a fanfare of harsh words, which meant no tantrums. Mother was satisfied she did not have to carry a child on her back in addition to a heavy load of yams and firewood on her head for three miles on the uphill trek to the village. Once the load was up on her head, we would continue, and sometimes, my hand would be held for most of the way.

Mother's ceremonious praising drew the attentions of others who were not as keen about praising children. Some might go to the extent of insinuating that I was pampered too much. Such comments would be my excuse for outbursts and tantrums. I might not get carried on her back, but at least I would settle for her holding my hand. It was my way of proving I was still in control; as the king I was still in charge.

I would cry, "Please hold my hand as we walk. Please hold my hand." Others might be so tired of hearing my whining and might even request to help as we walked up hill. It was a no-brainer to reject their gestures, because they were not my mother.

"No! No" was the answer for those meddlers who provoked my anger when they called out that I was pampered.

Such over-dependence began to be reshaped from the curious sense of seeing other boys my age act like brave little guys. Their mothers did not hold their hands. Some mothers had boys or little girls carry heavy loads as they walked along. I realized Mother was kinder to me, after all.

The more I observed others, the more I began to withdraw within myself during those situations with Mother and her friends. I joined the boys, who went to the secluded areas. The adults talked in idioms that it was expected for "a child of a person" to do these things, as in the saying, "a bit of wisdom was told to a child." It didn't sink in until one of the elders—the school principal, Iluore of Iyora—said to me, "Tears will wash your beauty away from your face." It was a way of saying, "The one who was born rich still cries for money." His words conveyed in essence what Mama had been saying all along, that "a child does not cry for nothing's sake!"

The lowering crescendo of my feigned crying might explain our culture and family relationships. We lived in this large family and everyone had to assume some responsibilities. "Eramha has responsibilities to everyone in the family," Mama said. "We don't take things for granted. Don't be fooled that someone will take care of you. Everyone must fend for themselves. You must understand that you shouldn't expect your older family members to neglect the responsibilities of raising their own children in order to take care of you."

Baba Akhamie Osigwe (Patriarch)
Akhamiemona of Afowa –Uzairue

Out of respect, a married woman did not call her husband by name. Mama called our father Eramha. The village elders, as heads of households, were also called Eramha. I felt it was awkward, especially as far as the women's roles were concerned, but I realized it was a good way to instill respect.

Also as part of the culture, a child was not expected to stay dependent for long. A child was expected to earn a badge of courage; such was the case with me. Mama pushed me away from her bosom—cut the apron strings—before I was enrolled in school. I was glad, because the boy who hid under his mother's bedcovers was seen as weak and unprepared for life.

Afowa-Uzairue

The village of Afowa has tall beautiful trees, and the surrounding jungle is majestic. There is a reserved area of grassland called an adevo. Traditionally, the grass straw was taken from there and woven into sheets for roofing our houses. There are natural mineral deposits such as kaolin—or kaolinite—around the adevo, and the fine, quicksand-like soil cannot sustain the growth of deep-rooted, tall trees.

Afowa is at the top of a hill, and the people have planted many varieties of fruit trees side by side with ornamental trees. After many years the parade of trees in the village provides shade from the heat of the tropical sun, as cool breezes come and go like majestic fans.

From the village, we would go to the farms and along the way meet at Ugholomi, which was the ever-present scene of childhood and where we engaged each other in the sport of wrestling and other play. Before getting exposed to schooling or the experience of a formal education, Ugholomi was the training ground for many activities. Equally inspiring, however, was the huge Catholic missionary center which had taken root in Uzairue.

The clan of Uzairue in Etsako—meaning the people with split teeth—is a subgroup within the Edo tribe. Unlike the bigger tribes in Nigeria—such as the Ibo, Hausa, and Yoruba—Edo does not have one language. The clan of Uzairue has nineteen villages— Afashio, Afowa, Apana, Ayoghena, Ayua, Ayoguiri, Elele, Idato, Ikabigbo, Ikholo, Imeke, Irekpai (Ivhihekhai), Ivhiorha (Iyora), Iyamho, Iyukhu, Jattu (Ikpe), Ogbido, Ugbenor, and Uluoke. The central town is Ikpe-Jattu, where the clan head resides. Ogieneni is the title of the clan head, and he is often praised with the title of Izaki.

The lands of the Uzairue clan are in the shape of a fan, with Jattu located at the base. The historical origin has been traced to its progenitors, who were mostly warriors and hunters from the Bini kingdom. History is taught by word of mouth, and through this oral history, teachers at the elementary schools teach their students about the Uzairue.

There are no particular distinguishing attributes of the Uzairue in Etsakor. Jattu is the center of commercial and cultural activities in the Uzairue clan. In addition to it being the home of the clan head, it is also where the major market is situated. From stories, I have learned that Uzairues prize a beautiful smile as a virtue, which led to the people etching a gap between their front teeth. Even in present day, the importance of a bright, beaming smile when conveying greetings of recognition is respected. In fact the name Etsakor—which means "those with the split"—came from the traditional practice of teeth filing." We are proud of our cultural identity, but the custom of filing teeth was discarded before my time.

Our tradition embraces the belief that our elders have the wisdom of knowledge and know the stories of our heritage. In gathering the stories for this memoir, I reached out to my older siblings, who were able to collect stories and information from the elders scattered throughout the clan. There is an African saying, "The youth walks faster, but elder knows the road."

My oldest brother, Peter, told the story of our ancestors going back into the period when the white man first came to the Uzairue clan. "Before the European missionaries took root in Uzairue, many were suspicious of the intentions of the white man. The oyibo visitors were welcomed, but the Uzairue people did not allow the visitors to settle at Jattu town. Instead, they gave them the jungles and burial grounds between Afashio, Afowa, and Jattu, which allowed the Uzairue people to keep an eye on the white man's activities. There was one hunter from Uluoke who escorted the Portuguese explorers as they traveled to the surrounding areas of Afemai province. He was called Osigwe Okhuru—he was my late grandfather.

Afowa Village scene

OSIGWE OKHURU, MY GRANDFATHER

I do not have much knowledge of my grandpa, who died many years before any of my siblings were born. The family did not use his name as their surname. From the stories Mama used to tell, I learned that he was a native of Uluoke, which is one of the villages in Uzairue, located 140 kilometers from Benin along the Benin-Okene Highway.

Peter travelled to Uluoke and several villages within Uzairue to ask questions of living relations about our roots at Uluoke. Peter found that our grandfather, Osigwe, had two wives, Okhee (also Orkhe or Orkheh)—meaning "wanting something"—who is our grandmother, and another wife who had a daughter called Aregimhe; therefore, that wife was known as "the mother of Aregimhe Osigwe."

Osigwe had two children: a son called Momoh, who was born to Okhee, and the daughter called Aregimhe from the other wife. (We have no knowledge of her name). However, Aregimhe gave birth to Arunah, who resided at Uluoke.

Osigwe was light skinned and hefty. A renowned hunter and

known for bravery in his days, Grandpa's personal talents allowed him to serve the European explorers, particularly within the Igalla kingdom. During the expeditions, Osigwe left his family in the family compound in Uluoke with his brother Ogbazi and others. The family at that time consisted of Okhee and her son, Momoh, who was my father. "Momoh" was the name given at birth to my father by my grandfather.

In the early 19th century, there were no paved roads, only winding footpaths. Also, there were no means of communication: no postal services, telegraphs, or telephones. People travelled by foot and horses and had minimal contact with people from other tribes. Osigwe was said to have gone with the Europeans for years, meaning a complete absence from home.

The traditional Nigerian customs are at their best when it comes to caring for extended family members. Family members all build their houses in a particular location and they all have a common surname. When a man had the means to build his own compound to house himself, his wife or wives, and all the children, he could move to a virgin forest and establish a village that would bear his name. The practice of polygamy was encouraged because the wealth and success of a man was measured by the number of children he sired.

Osigwe had siblings—Ogbazi and others—who were expected to take care of Okhee and her son while Osigwe was away fighting alongside the Europeans. But the realities were far from that, as the young, tender, frail boy Momoh was bullied by his uncles and their children. He was sickly and his body was often covered with a skin rash. He was the only child of his mother, Okhee, who had problems becoming pregnant because of an irregular menstrual cycle. Then, that was a problem indeed! In the complete absence of modern medicine, such abnormality could not be corrected. How I wish she were still alive to see her great-grandchildren, among whom are medical doctors treating such cases.

As an only child, Momoh was the treasure of his mother. Hence, she referred to him "*Akhamie mona,*" meaning "this one will not be taken from me."

Matriarch and Grandmother (Uwewe)
Orkhee Osigwe

My grandmother was called Uwewe, meaning "mother of all." My real contact with her began when I was old enough to run errands around the house. Mama, as the caretaker and provider, would send Philip and me to deliver food to Uwewe in her room. In Akhamie's household, she was Uwewe, meaning "mother–mother for everyone." Uwewe's real name was Okhee (pronounced Okhay, Okhaie, or Orkhay). That was the name Baba—my father—called her and that was how we found out her real name. Okhee means "the one who seeks."

We all belonged to her because of her position as the matriarch, a progenitor with direct lineage to our Afowa ancestry. There is a compelling reference that she was a feminist in her time.

We knew little in the case of her husband, my grandfather Osigwe. He died well before my generation was born, and nothing has been preserved in writing about him.

Okhee carries the honor of founding our large family. Momoh, her only child, married four wives and fathered 17 children who survived to adulthood. Akhamie and Okhee lived for many years, well into the modern era. They are the beginning of the family dynasty established in Afowa; a dynasty which has gained fame that reverberates to other villages. Okhee wielded a lot of influence.

In her youthful days, Okhee was described as slender, slim, and tall. She was endowed with beauty and brilliance, which were the traits that attracted Osigwe Okhuru, one of the famous hunters at that time and a native of Uluoke. Osigwe's family held the reigning chieftainship of Uluoke as direct descendants or heirs to the throne. Osigwe's brother Agbazi was the chief of Uluoke.

When Okhee was a young woman, custom permitted the royals, who had both wealth and influence, to travel throughout the Uzairue kingdom to find dignified wives. It was a distance of one day's journey along foot trails from Uluoke to Afowa. The men traveled on horses; only the wealthy could afford such privileges. Therefore, those who traveled outside of their villages were the well-to-do and could afford the bride price. Young girls old enough to be married into well-off, polygamous families often brought exorbitant bride prices. This customary practice of polygamy created an artificial scarcity of single females.

Okhee often told stories about how she left Uluoke. One such story concerns the period after the birth of her son, Akhamie (who was named Momoh at birth). She told story in her own words and it has been passed down as oral history.

> *I wanted desperately to have another child, more children. We were trying. I seem to have the problem of getting pregnant. At one time I spoke in confidence into the attentive ears of Chief Okhu from Okpella, who often stayed with my in-laws and family on his journeys to and from Ikpe-Jattu to conduct business or sell goods at the Uzairue market. Okhu, from the royal household of Okpella, traveled on a horse and knew about native medicine. Okhu promised to bring the pregnancy potion made of herbs from his land. For the potion to work properly, it had to be prepared in a delicious dish and eaten together by the wife and husband before going to sleep.*
>
> *On the day I prepared the dish, I waited for my husband in my hut at his regular time to show up for dinner. The food got cold, and I waited until I was virtually starved. Finally, well past dinnertime, I went to his hut. I opened the mat door and found my husband in bed with another woman. I reacted violently. I grabbed the calabash barrel full of honey and smashed it on them.*
>
> *It was an abomination, an offense which deserved severe punishment. My husband loved me. He said that he could not think of any punishment for me since he knew that he was wrong for taking the other woman to bed. Although he was wrong, what I did was considered a dishonor to the family because the man was not to be blamed. My mother-in-law (Ogbaih) went to the king, Oghieneni of Uzairue, and declared she did not want me in the household.*
>
> *A married woman could run away from the husband's house to her parents'. If there was an issue of bride price, especially if there was no child, the parents were required to return the bride price to the husband and his family. If there were no children, it would be assumed that the husband had already gained a profit from the marriage.*

Women belonged to the husband's household. Any man who was not able to enforce dominion over the wife was looked upon as a weak man. A man with only one wife was also seen as weak. So my husband and I were pressured by his mother to bear more children, and he was pressured to marry more women.

At Ikpe-Jattu, the king dispatched his guards (Ifai mia no-Oba). When they arrived at Uluoke, I left with my baby, which is how the name "Akhamie mona" came about, since I insisted that they could not take from me this one. They walked me through the village and to my village at Afowa.

It was market day, people were traveling to the big market, and my attention was drawn by the sound of loud shouts in the distance. As we looked behind us, there appeared to be someone in the distance coming towards us. As we continued to walk, the people shouted more and pointed at a man who was motioning to us to stop. After a brief moment, I saw that the man was my husband, who had caught up with us. He traveled with us on the remaining journey to Afowa.

My husband assured me that he would not abandon me and his son. Since I was banished from his village, he did not have any choice but to come along and stay with me. I believed my husband, who was quite persuasive as one could be who has traveled to distant places. After weighing his options of staying at Afowa in lieu of forfeiting his royal status, my husband decided to abandon his birth right and start over with me at Afowa.

My grandmother Uwewe Okhee died in 1971. She was buried at a designated spot near her room. When she died, she was laid in state in one of the rooms where I used to play in Mama's bungalow. I was afraid of her dead body and did not want to go there for months after she was buried.

One day Mama sent me to go and fetch something from there. Not admitting that I was scared of Grandma's corpse, I went to the room but decided to rush back outside. I was not paying attention as the door swung closed and the back of my left heel caught in between the closing door and flame. I was in pain as I returned to Mama. Being shamed and reluctant to be seen as weak, I didn't tell anyone about the injury. The pain my Achilles tendon—and the scar the injury left—taught me a lesson: beware of irrational fears and ignorance. Not asking questions made for one a foolish child.

By the time my grandma Okhee died, the whole matter about Uluoke had become less of a concern. Maybe Father felt he would return there to reclaim his inheritance. But with time he maintained less and less contacts, although the family often travelled to Uluoke to farm our portion of land. Father may have pointed out the gravesite of Grandpa Osigwe to others in the family, but I have never travelled there.

Baba inherited the distinctive characteristics of strength and determination. As an enterprising man, he travelled to many places, riding on his bicycle throughout southern Nigeria from the Niger-Benue area of Bida-Lokoja to the coastal Bight of Bini. He often told stories of Osimile, the big river Niger, and Oku, the Atlantic Ocean. Baba, describing the waves, said, "Oku's waves rose high like a huge fog of soap, the waves rose up higher and higher and came crashing on the shore."

Grandma Uwewe Okhele was always protective of her only child until she passed. Any little illness of her son would trigger the counteraction of seeking guidance from the oracles. Baba's grandchildren were becoming parents of their own, but Grandma Okhee still believed that her son had to be protected from evil forces who could do him harm. There were many stories about Grandma's over-protection. One story was that the oracles forbid contact between Akhamie and his half-sister. Many in the family did not know of the half-sister's existence and recognized Akhamie as the only child.

Another story that was peculiarly eerie involved an Afowa man of divinity, a priest of the oracle called Inene. The priest, who wielded total influence over the villagers through divinations, was respected by many. Upon consultation with the oracles, he instructed that one of the finest goats in Akhamie's herd be sacrificed at the altar of Inene. Grandma obliging said, "I am eager to provide anything Inene asks!" When Baba returned from the farm, his mother told him that the goat had been given as a sacrifice to Inene. Although he was upset, Baba said nothing to his mother.

On another day the priest returned and said that the oracle wanted the biggest sheep from the herd. Okhee, who was an unwavering follower, felt obliged, and the sheep was taken away to be killed. Again, Baba said nothing. A third animal was taken; he said not a word of protest to his mother.

On the Uzairue market day, Baba and his sons went to the Uzairue market. As they went around, they saw the sheep and goats they had given to Inene were on sale. Baba called his sons and said, "Untie the animals and take them home."

A goat knows its owner and it was returned to its original home.

"No harm will happen!" Baba said.

Baba, who was always calm in demeanor, held onto his beliefs, for it was well-known that the oracle would not harm one who was the true owner and did not give willingly.

The Life and Dynasty at Afowa

It was a matter of concern regarding our families' ties at Uluoke, but through research of our family history, Peter discovered that, "Years ago, the family's decision and action marked the beginning of an irreversible journey that can be likened to the biblical movement of Abraham from Haran to the Promised Land."

Our grandfather and grandmother never went back to Uluoke after the marital conflicts that caused their relocation to Afowa.

Our grandparents could have separated or divorced. But in those days, and up until the recent era, divorce was not encouraged. This was due to the significance of marriage in our society. However, disputes during the marriage could be irreconcilable, as in the case of Osigwe's family and Okhee. Ugbai (the mother-in-law) took the matter to the court of Chief Omogbai, the clan head of Uzairue, at Ikpe, paid the necessary fee, and the marriage was dissolved. She came home with one of Chief Omogbai's palace guards, who enforced the order. Okhee had no voice, no support; she could only comply. She packed her few possessions and took her son, saying, *"Akha mhie mona,"*—meaning, "they can't take this one from me."

Osigwe made the unusual decision—for a man—to settle with his wife and son at Afowa. Peter saw it as a reflection from the Bible and said, "Thus, he forsook his second wife and her daughter, leaving them at Uluoke. Like Abraham, he forsook his father's house, his kindred, and his ancestral inheritance with royalty at Uluoke for the love of his wife and the son, the only son."

Afowa, which is located about 10 km (6.2 miles) from Uluoke (and about 10 km, 7 miles) east of Auchi, was well-suited for our family. The chieftaincy resides in the Imokhai's family, which has always been hospitable to strangers, more so to any person born in the village, irrespective of their origin. It is because of this comfort and acceptance that visitors found it easy to settle in the village. Many families that settled in Afowa in the later part of the 19th century have similar testimonies.

Akhamie with Four Wives at the Household at Afowa

Grandpa Osigwe and Father carved out their compound and went on to create their identity under the name of Akhamie, since they were resolved not to return to Uluoke. One may be wondering why it was known as Akhamie's compound and not Osigwe's. And why the use of Akhamie as the family's last name? As tradition dictated, since Akhamie was the son of one of the daughters of Afowa, he had the rights and privileges which his father did not possess, even after he had "naturalized." In other words, no one could challenge Akhamie and his descendants over their estates at Afowa.

Grandpa Osigwe took his wife and son and moved away from his in-law's house to settle on the outskirts of the compound. He pitched his hut at the eastern outskirts of the in-law's compound. The villagers were superstitious and believed evil spirits inhabited the outskirts of the nearby forest. As such, it was not a choice location, since it was close to the in-law's refuge dump, and beyond the dump to the south was impenetrable virgin jungle people dared not enter. The villagers declared the enchanting jungle as the "no go" area, due to prevailing beliefs. Contrary to those beliefs, Osigwe and Akhamie took on the jungle, cutting down the *Iroko*—gigantic trees also known as *Uloko*—for timber and transformed the jungle into farmland.

Iyawo Etaitsikhe Akhamie—First Wife

When Father came of age, his parents went to Uluoke to get a teenage girl named Iyawo Etaitsikhe for him to marry. In those days, girls as young as five years old could be given in marriage. They were expected to grow up in the husband's house, under the tutelage of the would-be mother-in-law.

Grandpa Osigwe wanted his son to maintain his paternal roots by marrying someone from Uluoke. However, Grandma (Uwewe), because of the unpleasant experiences with her in-laws, didn't want to take the chance of getting an unsuitable girl to marry her only child. For Grandma, such a girl must be nurtured by none other than herself. Iyawo happened to be that girl. Thus she was the first wife.

When Iyawo was finally old enough to formally assume the role of a wife, she gave birth to Akhamie's fourth child, a son, who was called Albert Umoru.

By the time I was growing up, Iyawo was very old and had lost her sight, so she spent most of her time inside her house. I could not have much interaction with her because of her feisty nature; however, her only child, Albert Umoru—who had been living in Lagos since before I was born—was my favorite senior brother at the time. From Lagos, Albert Umoru sent money home to build the corrugated, zinc-roofed house in the spot where the old hut house had been demolished.

Iyawo had done many things when she lived in the hut house, where she would cook and share food with the children. As she got older, it seemed she grew less kind, because she cursed a lot whenever she heard that someone travelled to Lagos to stay with Albert Umoru. She was the first among the wives to pass on, and her house remained unoccupied for a long time.

Brother Albert Umoru (deceased)
Albert Umoru was the only son born to Iyawo.
Albert went to reside in Lagos in the 1950s.
He raised his family in Lagos

Sister Anima (married to Mr. Etu)
Died on February 14, 2017
Anima is the first daughter of Akhamie. She married Etu and has outlived many of her age group. Among her children is Columbanus (Captain Banus) who joined the Nigerian military as a young man about the time of Biafra war and rose to the rank of captain.

Beatrice Ayemekhulu (deceased)
Beatrice Ayemekhilu was married to William Uloko. Uloko was one of Akhamie's closest friends. William and family lived in Ibadan where some of the children grew up. However, Ayemekhulu possessed the character of a tough woman and owned the land on the outskirts of the village. That land is where her first son Thomas Uloko constructed the first modern guesthouse/hotel in the village

Brother Anabi Ogiorumua (deceased)
The second born son of Akhamie; "Anabe" as he liked to be called was the radical one with free spirit. He assumed the leadership of the family after the death of Agbierere. He farmed the family lands referred to Agenebode and acquired his own lands in the vicinity of Ederaerue. He practiced herbal medicine and artisan craftsman. Among his grandchildren include a medical doctor

Sametu Idakhe (Isametu (or Isatu) Akhamie)—Second Wife

Before Iyawo could grow to maturity, it was said that a terrible incident happened which made Akhamie take a full-grown girl as his second wife. There was the sudden death of one of Akhamie's maternal cousins, who left behind his young wife. The widow, a very beautiful, fair-skinned girl, was called Isametu (nicknamed Isatu), and she was a native of Ogbido in the Uzairue clan.

The tradition was for one of the brothers or kinsmen of the diseased to marry the widow. The lot fell on Akhamie, and he had to marry Isametu as his second wife. In no time she gave birth to a son, Akhamie's first child, who was named Agbirere. This was followed by a girl named Anima, then a son named Ogieorumua (Alabi, Anabi,). Sametu Idakhe's fourth child, a girl, was named Ayemhekulu.

I knew Isatu as one of the liveliest people ever. As a young boy I thought I could wrestle, so she would straddle me in a make-believe wrestling match while I held onto her legs with all my energy. She was about five feet five inches tall but slightly heavy —although not considered fat—and had a very fair complexion. Isatu did not have any qualms about name-calling and provoking fights; everyone stayed clear of making trouble with her. Everyone, including her grandchildren, called her by her nickname of Isatu, but when she wanted to tangle with someone, she preferred—depending on her mood—to be called Apekhe, which essentially meant "small troublemaker."

As she grew older, she became tougher to deal with and she quarreled with nearly everyone. When she talked over the fence with her partner-wife Iyawo, it was rather amusing and entertaining. They both had lost their sight but would yell at each other from their separate homes. They sang old songs of insults, but Isatu was more provocative and would walk a long way to instigate trouble with the other women. Everyone simply ignored them. Sometimes the arguments would carry on into the night. At other times the third wife got involved, and one of them would instigate trouble with her by singing songs of insults.

As I grew into my teenage years, I did shy away from personal contacts with Isatu, since it was believed to be a bad omen for the old women to be using the names of the young children in their songs.

IMAETU OSHIOMHIEBO—THIRD WIFE

Imaetu Oshiomhiebo was Akhamie's third wife. She was a native of Apana, which is within the Uzairue clan. We called her by the nickname, Imaatu. She had six children: four boys and two girls, in the following order: Amedu, Akhalumhe Boniface, Ughiarekha Moses, Imeghomhe (girl), Adekhe James and Irelomheme Abebi Victoria (girl).

For one reason or another, the story is that her dowry price was paid twice. First was Oriso, and after the birth of Moses Ughiarekha, her father proposed to Osigwe that he pay another dowry as *aimi,* meaning "birth-right." This amounts to "selling her," with no possibility of her ever returning to her kinsmen. Therefore, she was regarded as a daughter in her husband's home. Such marriages were usually contracted with women who were not from our clan, the Uzairue. They are called *aimioya*. It was after this that Imeghomhe, Adekhe, and Abebi were born; hence, they are called "sons of the soil" (*iviami or iviotoi*). Imaetu was a no-nonsense woman, just as Iyawo and Isatu. As such, they maintained bitter rivalries all through their lives.

I maintained a mother relationship with Imaatu—as we called her—especially since she was convinced I was endowed with certain inborn powers as the last-born child of the family. I often accompanied Baba to her house, which was located in a separate part of the village. Imaatu Akhamie height was about five feet eight inches tall and dark in complexion, similar to my mother's skin tone. She had a strong personality and was a hands-on person, which made her well suited as the matron who cared for new babies born in the household.

*Baba Akhamie's 3rd wife
Imaatu Oshiomhiebo*

*Brother
Amedu*

Brother (deceased)
Akhalumhe Boniface, "Ticha"

Brother (deceased)
Ughearekhai Moses

Brother
James Ayaochimhe Adeke (deceased)

Imegomhe Ikhalumhe

Imegomhe married Mr. Matthias Ikhalumhe of the village of Elele, Uzairue.

The family resided in Ibadan in Oyo state, where they raised their children. The daughter Rosalyn is married to Rev. Rufus Azeboje and they are both pastors (husband and wife) who have resided in Scotland where they pastor a church and raised their children. Rosalyn was the first of Akhamie grandchildren who resided in Europe and as such pioneered opening of new frontier for those descendants in Germany, Italy, Scotland and United Kingdom

*Sister Victoria Abebi
Married to Isaedu Ikhumetse*

AMINA CELINA AKHAMIE—FOURTH WIFE

My mother was the fourth wife. By tradition at the time, all the wives were regarded as our mothers but were usually called by the nicknames they preferred. Mama—many called her Amina—was not as feisty as the others. She was a native of the Ogute village in the Okpella clan, the eastern boundary of Etsako. She was known as *onabor* and *aimi,* meaning "daughter of the soil by virtue of marriage from a different clan." She had five children, four boys and one girl: Agbokhiavho Paul, Aneke Omoaluna Cecilia, Agbasovhelo Peter,

Phillip Ikhane, and me, David Ekhalevhe Aleghe.

Mother was only in her teens when she married my father, so she actually grew up in our house, where she was raised as a child-bride. But remarkably dutiful to her husband and never walked out on her mother-in-law, whom she took as her mother.

When Christianity took a firm root in the village, Mother became a Pentecostal and was one of the first to be born again at Afowa in the 1960s. She never regarded the other three women as her friends, some of whom were old enough to be her mother. She died on September 15, 1990, at the estimated age of 60.

Iyawo	Isametu	Imaetu	Amina
Umoru Albert	Agbirere Idirisu	Amedu	Agbokhiavho Paul
	Anima (married Luke Etu Igudu)	Akhalumhe Boniface	Aneke Cecilia Omoaluna (married Gregory Idodo)
	Anabi (Alabi) Ogieorumua	Ugharehka Moses	Agbasovhelo Peter
	Ayemhekhulu Beatrice (married William Uloko)	Imiegomhe (married Ikhalumhe)	Phillip Ikhane
		Adekhe Ayaochimhe James	Ekhalevhe Aleghe David
		Abebi Victoria (married Isaedu Ikhumetse)	

Chart of the families of Father's four wives

Mama's personality was well suited for the role she played as the youngest of the four wives. She took care of Baba as well as the other wives when they could not do for themselves in their old age. She would cook and share with the other wives whenever she found they were missing meals. She did not involve herself in the ongoing rivalries among the others and maintained a pleasant demeanor as she followed the teachings of Jesus Christ.

The Land and Farms of Akhamie

My father came to Afowa at a time when land was in abundance and seemed inexhaustible. The virgin jungle forest was impenetrable and intimidating. It was only the bold and courageous who could confront it and exploit its hidden treasures. Land ownership was determined on the basis of who first cleared the virgin forest and farmed on that land. Once one farmed the land, it automatically became that person's farmland.

As a self-starter at Afowa, in order to secure land for farming, Father had no choice other but to claim part of the dreaded forest around the village. Akhamie disregarded—and taught his children to ignore—the fearful stories told about the occupants of the jungle who, he said, were mere fable and hunters' tales. He assaulted the jungle, cut down 100-year-old Iroko and mahogany trees, and conquered the forest as far as he could go, which was evident based on the large expanse of fertile farmland he claimed. These properties became his three farms, which were referred to as Okhotorgba, Agenegbode and Okhotoime (an area referred to as Iyahdi at Afowa).

The Gardens

The word *ogba* means "garden" in Afemai. Okhotogba was the family land closest to the compound, and it extended to the border between the Afowa and Afashio villages. The first of Akhamie's farms was used as the family's garden. Okhotogba means "the deep down garden." The original jungle was comprised of many Iroko trees—one tree cannot make a forest—centuries old, and the undergrowth was inhabited by dangerous reptiles, wild cats, giant snails, etc. The undergrowth was carpeted with decaying leaves and dead, organic substances—which could be a foot thick—and mined with thorns as long as six feet (*aminua*).

The tall Irokos, mahogany, and other gigantic trees blocked sunlight in the forest and caused darkness in the daytime. The jungle was wet and moist, even in the dry season; hence, it was a safe haven for dreaded animals. Even demons were reputed to be living there.

At that time even the super-rich could not afford the luxury of wearing sandals (*ikhatakpo*) to ceremonial festivals or events and markets. In those days people went about bare footed, and a horse was a symbol of wealth and affluence. Those were the days when the best wedding gift a family could give was the bride's ride on horseback to her husband's compound on their wedding day.

As a young man, Baba Akhamie paid little attention to the dangers and myths about the jungle, for all that he saw was a fertile soil that would be suitable for growing vegetables, perennials, and cash crops. He saw timber that could fetch handsome cash rewards and the jungle beasts would be a source of protein to feed a growing family. Akhamie invaded the jungle, cutting it down acre by acre. There is a saying: he "takes one step at a time when mashing palm fruits in a mortar."

Akhamie did not bother himself with the massive, tall, and threatening century-old trees in the forest, although some of the trees were objects of worship and were treated as shrines throughout the villages. While the villagers revered the mystique of the jungle, Akhamie knew he had no inheritance waiting for him, and he decided to conquer the land. Another explanation was that he could have been influenced by his father's exposure to the white man, which helped to demystify the practice of worshipping jungle trees out of reverence to the gods.

Baba was biding his time, waiting for his son Agbirere to come of age. Agbirere became a sawyer in his twenties. He then decided to move to a new location when the land at Okhotogba began showing signs of distress. Baba and Agbirere planted rubber trees on the land or reserved it for the women for farming groundnuts, beans, sugarcane, and vegetables. Notable among the cash crops they planted was the cherry tree, called *oche osigwe*.

Everyone recounted the family's story of events that happened before I was born. The stories claimed that Akhamie's children, specifically his sons, were known for their knack of creativity and mental tenacity. Akhamie was a powerful force during his prime. There were many stories from my siblings regarding how he traveled to distant cities, riding on a bicycle—the iron horse—as a trader. The remnants and frame of that old, rugged iron horse lay for years in the cellars of the compound and served as testimonies of his youthful adventures. In those days, only the wealthy could afford an iron horse.

Agenegbode Farms

This farm was located about five kilometers north of Afowa. Baba had his rubber plantation there, as well as other cash crops like pear (*olomi*) and *ogi*. The vegetation was a mixture of grassland and rain forest; therefore, a variety of crops like beans, groundnut, and yams were cultivated. The grassland section of the farm (*atuaki*) was less fertile for growing yams, so it was allocated to the women to plant groundnuts, beans, sugar cane, peppers, and cassava. The women were expected to use the proceeds from their farm to feed the children and their husband. The women also harvested and sold some of the crops at the Uzairue market to generate funds for the family.

The men grew yams in the more fertile acres of the farm. Yams are one of our staple foods. Pounded yam with groundnut (peanut) soup was the men's favorite food. The ability to cook spiced groundnut soup was one of the yardsticks of knowing whether a girl had been properly brought up in the Etsako clan. This is true even today. So if a girl desires to marry an Etsako man, to win his heart, try serving him pounded yam-and-groundnut soup!

Our father passed on the tradition of farming to all his children, boys and girls alike. The children's first experience was learning survival skills by working on the farms with their parents. The boys, including the grandchildren, were all duty bound by tradition to follow Baba, as we referred to Father, on the farm. My elder brother Anabi would sometimes call Father by his first name—Akhamie. Anabi wanted to keep an independent view. He was one of two of Baba's 17 children who could act contrary to Baba's views or wishes.

In the household, I learned to keep close to my mother once Philip went to learn tailoring. I learned to keep my feelings, emotions, and fears under control, based on what I learned from my parents and brothers and sisters. I felt like I was swallowed up in the huge family of relatives. There were just too many family members to interact with, so I decided to stay closer to Mother, where I felt safe.

Peter Agbasovhelo

I was about seven when Peter left home to attend secondary school at St. John Secondary School at Fugar in the Avianwu clan. He spent the holidays at home, and when he was ready to depart for school, he called Philip and me to help carry his luggage to the motor park located at Jattu. Peter told me, "David, you carry this one. I will meet you there. Do not leave my bag alone until I get there. Go ahead now."

Peter helped us to lift and balance the loads carefully on our heads, and we walked to the motor park at Jattu. After a walk of about two miles, we were in the middle of Jattu. The attendants at the motor park—they were called *agbero*—shouted out the destination as they loaded the taxi while the driver took a break somewhere.

"Avianwu, Okpella, Bode!"

"*Na whe yu dey go?*" the agberos would ask.

Apprehensive about the hustling, we ignored them and waited for Peter, who suddenly appeared.

Agberos shouted, "Fugar, one to go! No waiting!" They hustled travelers to load the taxis.

The young men referred to as agberos did not attend school; instead, they ran the streets, hustling to make quick money, which they spent like fugitives on the run. They got paid after they loaded luggage and packages and collected the fares from passengers.

As the years went by, Peter became more studious and quieter in manner. He had grown taller as a teenager and had long, Afro hair.

I recalled how Peter used to carry me on his back when I was a baby. I liked his kind heart—like our Mother's—and wanted to grow up to be like him. Peter was smart and reserved as a young adolescent. Whether it was the native name Agbaso—meaning "life is good"—or the charming smile or his mild manners, Peter was well liked by everyone, and he was very social and caring, again like our Mother. I obliged whenever he sent me on "sneaky errands" to pass notes to his female friends.

I wondered about his instruction—"Don't open it"—since I could not read even if I opened the notes. I got better than Philip as a decoy, so Peter relied on me to do errands through word of mouth without resorting to writing his pensive notes. Those were the days when telephones were unavailable in Uzairue.

Peter was easy going but did outstanding at school. He was intuitively driven in making choices and participated in many church activities. He seemed ahead of his time and uninhibited in expressing love for the family and stood firmly as a "rock," like one at the middle of the bridge holding things together.

Much later, Peter obtained his higher education at universities in Russia—during the Soviet Union era—and then returned to Nigeria. Peter and I had a mutual interest in history, so we coordinated our efforts to recover our family's stories. Peter undertook the oral research by asking questions of the elders and relatives throughout Uzairue. He recounted some of own his personal experiences as a young man before I was born.

Peter "Agbaso" Agbasovhelo

Peter's Story

The *oche Osigwe* (cherry tree of Osigwe) was a massive tree located about one fourth of a mile from my father's compound. As stated previously, Osigwe was my grandfather, whom I did not know personally. Presumably, the cherry tree grew wild in the jungle, and Grandfather was the first to farm around it, or maybe it was just planted. Irrespective of the origin, I grew up to respect the tree as one of the family's treasured landmarks bearing my grandfather's name.

This massive tree covered an area as wide as one quarter of a football field. It was over 50 meters (160 feet) tall and was supported by huge root buttresses. It produced fruit annually from November to April. During that period, school-age children and youths spent most evenings and weekends around it. The youths would throw sticks (*ubaba*) to pluck the ripe fruit from the tree.

The children and "stubborn" girls usually hung around, waiting to scramble for any fruit that fell naturally. The descent of ripe fruit yielding to gravity would be announced by a sound. The attentive would hear as it fell through the leaves, colliding with branches while falling from heights of about 30 to 50 feet. There was expectation during the two to three seconds of descent, and then the contest for the fruit when it hit the ground was like a tackle in American football. The roughness and mad dashing for the cherry prevented most of the girls from getting involved in the contest. Only the toughest of the "stubborn" girls would fight for the prize. More so, it was generally accepted that women were not to be seen competing with men. Girls were supposed to stay around their mothers, learning how to cook and manage the home.

The big boys would climb and harvest cherries to sell in the market. It was possible for five people to climb one tree at the same time, each harvesting from separate branches. I braved the heights to climb the 30 feet height twice before I left home for secondary school.

Climbing the huge cherry tree was one of the first challenges a young man would face to present himself as strong enough to get married. Another was the skill to climb and harvest the fruits of a palm tree. It was an exercise in bravery, in the sense that no parent would openly approve of it because of the looming danger of death from a fall. In addition to the lofty heights, it was believed that evil spirits and ghosts dwelt around the trees.

In view of these beliefs, we were not encouraged to go there alone and were forbidden to go there at noon. For us it was fun to be there with friends, out from under the watchful eyes of our mothers, who would not miss any opportunity to "make girls out of boys" by assigning chores like washing plates and assisting in the kitchen. The general belief was that a man should not go to the kitchen. "A man who tastes the soup on the fire while it is still being cooked will not grow a beard." Thus was the clear warning for young boys to stay away from the kitchen.

The only girl among my siblings was Cecilia, called Emosi by our parents. We called her Aneke as a nickname. Her native name at birth was Omoaluna, meaning a "child we do for". She was married in 1963—right after she completed elementary school—to one of the school's young, aspiring teachers, my brother-in-law Gregory Idodo. Mama and Peter have recounted the story of her marriage many times. They said that it was arranged by Anabi—our older brother from Isaatu, the second wife—without Baba's knowledge.

Peter said, "Anabi knew quite well that Baba would not have approved of her marrying at that time. Baba wanted to send her to school."

Peter went on to explain that the suitor, who was a teacher, trusted Anabi since no one could convince Baba about the marriage. "So on a market day, Anabi arranged for her to elope," Peter said.

"When Baba found out, what happened?" I asked.

"Oh, he was very upset and would not eat for days, but knowing that it was Anabi who authorized the arrangement, he had to calm down about the whole thing."

"What about Mama? What did she do?" I asked.

"Mama was kind of aware of the arrangement and went along with it because she knew he was the right son-in-law for her daughter."

"Peter," I said, "you mean Mama would know about something and not talk about it with Baba?"

Peter explained, "Yes, Mama knew the ropes. She knew what she wanted and how to get along with Baba. You should never underrate how precocious she was! But she went into her room and cried because she was sad and she missed our sister."

Concerning the marriage of our sister, Cecilia Aneke to the Idodo family, Mama explained, "Sometimes, one has to play the role of a fool to get along and get something. Sometimes, if you let people know your mind, they are unwilling to give you what you want."

Chapter 2

The Biafra War

At about the age of five, it looked as if I was ready for primary school. Although skinny, I was taller than many kids in my age group. Without birth records, no one knew my exact age. However, I was enrolled in the village elementary school, called Demonstration Primary School, in January 1967. Every child who grew up in our house attended elementary school, so the conversations among the bigger boys was what happened at school, and they made jokes about the pitfalls they had heard about. During the year, I listened to many stories in amazement, wondering whether any snags would befall me. My nephew, who always had interesting stories about school, tried to instill fear.

There was a story about school that was circulated among the children by the older boys who had been to school. The theme behind such stories was to prevent us from making needless mistakes that dishonored the family. This story was about a senseless boy who went to school. Funny now, but deadly serious at the time. It was said that the teacher, taking attendance of first day at school, asked the boy, "What is your name?"

"Okpo!" the boy replied.

Okpo meant "boy" in the Uzairue dialect; it was every boy's name.

"What is your father's name?" the teacher asked.

"Baba," the boy told the teacher.

The wise teacher knew the boy and his parent but did not help him out, since it was believed that a child who learned the hard way learned faster.

"What was wrong with the answers he gave?" I inquired, wanting to be sure not to make such a mistake when I encounter my teacher.

"His father's name is not Baba," I was told. "Baba is every father. You must give the real name of your father—Akhamie. But the boy did not know his father's first or last name; he just called him Baba."

"Was he able to attend school?" I asked

"No, he was not. You have to be smart and be able to read and write; otherwise, you will fail. One who cannot pass cannot go school."

Therein lay the challenge I had to overcome in my first year of school: not knowing whether I would fail or pass. At that age all conversations were in our dialect of Uzairue, but the teacher—I do not recall his name—wrote on the blackboard with the chalk, and students practiced writing their numbers and letters—1-2-3s and a-b-cs—on slates.

Whenever I returned from school and listened to the conversations of my nephews, there were always stories and innuendos that instilled fear in me.

One of my nephews said, "If you think that school was tough, a long time ago, the white man (oyibo) decided whether the child was ready for school."

"What! You mean, the oyibo can tell whether one is ready for school?" I asked.

"Oh, yes!" said another nephew, who had heard the story before. "When the boys formed a line, the children were told to place their right hand across their head to touch their left ear. The ones who could not do it were told to go back home." The boy wrapped his right hand around the left ear easily. "You try it out now."

Could I have passed and been promoted, or would I have been stymied academically if I had stayed for the entire year? I wasn't sure and neither were my teacher nor classmates. I will admit that the war that year probably saved me from having to repeat primary grade one. I often asked myself, "How much did that event change my life?"

There had been rumors about the country going to war. As children we did not know much about the situation of the newly formed country of many tribal groups and its bid for independence from Great Britain. Although the news was on the radio and in newspapers, I did not know the war was coming or that it was caused by civil strife that originated among the various ethnic tribal groups. But I eventually came to realize that Nigeria was amalgamated from the major tribes of Ibo, Yoruba, and Hausa, other smaller tribes, and Edo. Within the tribes, the language, people, and culture were equally diverse, but the common language was English.

For children and the majority of masses who did not understood English, information was spread through rumors. At Afowa and every place around the country, rumors of war were buzzing, and people talked openly that the war had started in other parts of the country. This was heard on the radio, as well.

On one particular afternoon, we were told to leave school before regular dismissal time. Some responded to the early dismissal as if the soldiers were shooting. Some jumped out of the windows and ran towards the village. Others ran home and went to the farms to inform their parents that the war had reached us.

When the initial shock from the chaos had settled, we realized our school had been closed indefinitely. I wouldn't say that I missed out a whole lot, since the teaching in primary one was mostly focused on social interaction, learning numbers, and the alphabet. For the remainder of the school year, I went to the farm with my parents.

The villains of the war were the Biafra, who were mainly the ethnic group of Ibo-speaking people who occupied the southeastern part of Nigeria. The conflict involved the Ibo people not receiving fair treatment, being discriminated against, and other grievances which had morphed into the desire to secede from Nigeria and to have an independent nation of Biafra. The civil conflicts had resulted in the first bloody coup d'état, which was the military seizure of power and the killing of the country's rulers. Young military leaders were placed in positions of leadership: Chukwuemeka Odumegwu Ojukwu led the Biafra, and Yakubu Gowon—meaning "go on with one Nigeria"—led the combined forces of Hausa, Yoruba, and other ethnic groups that forced Biafra to surrender and keep Nigeria as one country.

The Biafra War started in July 1967 and officially ended in 1970. As a result of school closures, young men attending various higher institutions of learning returned to their respective towns and villages. Some of my nephews in the cities rejoined us at home. Everyone rallied around in the mornings to talk about the war.

Baba explained, "I have not experienced anything like this. There have been small conflicts here and there, but nothing of the magnitude of this civil war. Everyone has to be careful.

"My son Imodu, who lives in the city, joined the army. I heard the rumor, but I have not received any letters from him.

"Your sister Anima informed me that Icobani, who was in the army, has not been heard from, and no one knows whether he is okay.

"I will pray for the safe return of those who went to join the army. I will pray that no harm comes to them." *Ami Itse*! For those who are in school, there is no need to panic now. Everyone is safe here. The war is not going to last forever and those who should be in school will return when the schools are reopened. Ami Itse! No matter how bad things may look now, it will get better."

As I grew up with the experience of war at my young age, a close relationship evolved between my oldest sibling, Paul, and me. Baba expected Paul to shoulder the responsibilities of raising me, the youngest of the family.

Paul had already completed primary school when I was born and had reached his adolescent years. As such, he was given his own room on the second floor of our two-story building. As a teenager, he was tall and slim with head full of dark hair which he kept well-trimmed. A very handy person, he could cut his hair by himself within the confines of his room. He kept to himself at home but made friends with young people his age, which was his way of assuming authority as the leader and disciplinarian.

Paul Agbokhiavho
My oldest sibling

The strict disciplinary role over the house was a turn-off for many of us. I started expressing my concerns, first to Philip. I asked, "Why do you think Paul is so mean? Are you scared of Paul?"

Philip and I were both annoyed about our situation with Paul. Not knowing that Mama had already warned my older siblings that none of them should beat me, I complained to her that I did not feel that Paul, a sibling, should be *ogha* (meaning "the boss"). I wanted him to be my brother, not my dad or anything else!

Mama would say, "He is your brother, but you have to listen to what your elders tell you. Now do not worry about such things. You can call him 'brother' and be respectful."

For the older members of the family, Paul always conveyed the utmost respect as a polite young man, highly reliable, dependable, and trustworthy. Paul's friends admired our close resemblance. They said, "Paul, this boy looks just like you."

The likeness in looks, manners, and personality between Peter and me allowed me to develop a positive outlook and also a dislike for unyielding, stiff, spendthrift, self-focused people. With Paul it was a different matter, because he did not share his feelings but was self-focused to the point that we were withdrawn from each other.

My immediate senior brother, Philip, was about two years older than me. Philip disliked many things but liked the company of our nephews about his age. He did not stay around the kitchen with Mama and me. We fought each other when one of us felt cheated about something, but we were able to resolve our disputes and move on; we did not hold grudges for long.

Philip has a light-skinned complexion like Baba. Philip also has a nice smile but was forced to cover his mouth when his teeth were coming in. Even though we were only two years apart in age, we often engaged in rivalry because I often resented being the youngest. Philip hung with other members of the family, especially around our senior brother's parlor, where they talked about the flamboyant, good life.

Philip believed he would enjoy life since others were there for him to rely upon. Philip was smart but relied on the belief that he did not have to attend school to be successful. It was a false notion for lazy ones.

Philip

Philip had good looks as he became a teenager, but he was hampered because he had not stayed in school through the tough times and so did not finish elementary school. Philip believed that through his work as a tailor, he would make a good life for himself. He was impatient in learning and had only a basic, elementary education, but he was highly focused once he decided to learn tailoring.

Baba was disturbed that Philip had chosen not to attend school like the rest of us. In his usual solemn way, he said, "The child is expected to learn from the older ones, be respectful of their positions, and do as the others of his age group do." Baba would tell Philip that he had to do for himself. But Philip would not see that the family was warning him that no one would care for him when they were gone.

The family expressed their love for each other by their actions, but the word "love" is an abstract concept in our native dialect. But it was how Baba raised us, a way that was far superior to beating and screaming at a child.

I began early in life to actualize the meaning of Mama's saying, "Aspire beyond the ordinary," as if she knew that we would do great things.

She had a sincere love for her children, but there was a bitter taste in the home when Philip was going astray. "Philip, what is wrong with you?" she would ask. "Why don't you trust your family but rather run around to find others outside of our family?"

"Mama, there is nothing wrong with me?" Philip would answer back, but he spent most of his time with our relatives who did not attend school.

Already a grown man at the time, Paul did not talk much with us. He was focused on the job at hand—getting his own education was the one most important thing to him. His dogged focus was good, but the other side of that coin meant he was totally against the idea of marriage. After the war, Baba found him a young lady from Apana, but Paul rejected the idea of getting married.

He was the only one who owned a gramophone when, now and then, we celebrated something. We would gather in the parlor upstairs to listen to songs, but we kept our distance, careful not to be too close to the gramophone. He would put the vinyl record on the machine, twirl the handle to spin the record, and the sound to come out. Paul was far older than most of us and related to us more like an uncle than a sibling. It was an odd situation, since he was not married like most in his age group, and it was also disconcerting for our parents.

Both Baba and Mama wanted him to get married, but he was not ready. Such resolve was difficult for Mama, who longed to have a young woman to be with her as she aged quickly because of the hard life of toiling for the family. Every day she had to cook dinner—mostly pounded yam and Etsako soup—to be served to my dad, grandma, Paul, and Peter. Philip and I shared the dish with Dad. We could not help her much, as our own daily routines were overwhelming. Unlike the men, women toiled non-stop except when they slept. They were right back up in morning to repeat the strenuous work each and every day.

The void in Mama's life was more noticeable since our only sister, Cecilia, had married and moved out of the house. Baba did not complain, but Mama's pleas were taking their toll. She would say, "I have to do everything by myself. There is no one to help me!"

"What am I supposed to do?" I thought to myself as I tried to listen and not misbehave. "I am only a boy. I can't marry so that my wife can be with Mama."

Philip was nice and stayed around for a while but, as the war changed everything, he too was changed. For better or worse, Philip would take off and return as he liked. No one could keep him in check anymore.

Although the Biafra War was not fought in my village, any sightings of flying objects were enough to cause chaos, rumors, and confusion. A plane or helicopter must have flown close to the village one week when I went to visit my sister's house. The rumors must have spread like wild fire, as it seemed the people mistakenly thought the plane was dropping bombs. In that time of crisis and in the midst of confusion, people ran. Some were searching for family members.

Philip came over to meet me at our sister's place to report. He said, "For about three hours there, they were searching for you at home." He looked terribly frightened that war was coming, but my sister and her husband were not moved by the outward display.

"Follow Philip along so you can go home," my sister told me.

I realized that nothing was going on, but one of my older brothers had found his chance to make a nasty statement about me and my siblings while he pretended to be relieved that I was safe. He scolded, "You claim to know too much," which was an insinuation that I did not listen to my elders. My elder brothers did not want the burden and responsibilities of supporting my siblings and me, so everyone had to learn how to survive on their own.

Philip was gone by the time Mama explained why such comments were the nuances jealousy. Such things were not easy to convey, but one has to experience and learn from dealing with older brothers and sisters, with our father, and with the other wives.

"Don't worry about such things, but you have to understand they are serious, so you must learn to survive," Mama said.

For upwards of six months to a year, soldiers stayed in temporary barracks, which they commandeered along with the campus of the teachers training college annexed to the Demonstration Primary School. The college was called Assumption Teachers Training College. Many activities, especially educational facilities, were closed in most of the surroundings areas. Some of the young men from the village, including my nephews, went to join the military.

The federal soldiers were massed in the province bordering the eastern part of Nigeria. The main conflict, as everyone knew, was that the Ibos wanted a separate country called Biafra. From our village we heard loud gunshots coming from the eastern part of Nigeria. After the initial shock of the soldiers taking over control of that Etsako area had calmed down, everyone was made aware we are all going to remain as a united country. Hence, the soldiers were going to war to enforce the laws and to prevent the Ibos from breaking away into a separate country.

The Edo people during the Biafra Era were combined into one province called The Mid-western Province. It comprised all of the Afemai people and other ethnic groups who shared borders with the seceding Ibos. However, the Edos had been won over by the idea of peace and one nation, and they supported the "one Nigeria" concept.

In the villages, life was restored to normal daily activities: people and properties were spared, and we were freed. There was no school, however, so we ventured out to the school compounds to watch the soldiers at training, marching, and parades:

The solders dressed in battle gear and were armed with AK-45 rifles. One side would fight against the other in simulated battles. The "bad" side attacked and "good" side defended. They were shooting blanks, but the noise resembled live fire.

In other simulation training exercises, the soldiers would crawl from one spot to another with their rifles. I felt empathy for the new recruits, who had their heads shaved to the skull and who were often beaten with a *koboko* (whip) by the *kolofo* (the drill sergeant). That kolofo was the meanest SOB you could ever imagine. I was scared of the soldiers, who were big men with long rifles, but then, imagine the soldiers themselves, who were scared of the SOB kolofo. I kept my distance and cringed at the sight of the kolofo turning grown men into soldiers.

As one could imagine, social life was on the upswing. Motels, brothels, beer parlors, and eating places (*bukas*) were established at Jattu, as the business of entertainment sprang up as sources of income.

The young people from Uzairue, men and women, were discreet in engaging in the loose social life with the military men who came from other parts of the country. Some of the young women became *asawos* (prostitutes) and stayed at the motels. There were fights, but the soldiers had the upper hand in beating up the young men of the village.

Prior to the war, everyone farmed the land, and agriculture and related industries were the main economic sources. The rice processing mill was located at Jattu where road branched off to Okpella to the cement factory and onward to the north. During the drumbeats of chaos, the country fell into dismal, immoral decadence. There were reports of armed robberies, kidnappings, and ritualistic killings. There were persistent rumors about the consumption of human flesh. However, like the superstitious belief of witchcraft, I wondered whether people were really killed and their body parts sold in the markets. What about the families of the victims? No one close to me witnessed such evil things, but the rumors were everywhere.

The military restored order and imposed discipline on the nation. The serious crimes were handled by firing squad, and the pictures were posted in the newspapers as a lesson for everyone. Gradually, the heinous rumors faded as the country accepted its people as human beings, no matter what part of the country or ethnic group a person was from.

The Biafra War altered "everything and everyone," and the impact from the momentum of revolution has not slowed. The songs being sung were about militant themes, heroes and villains, you name it; everything was geared towards one unified theme which was broadcast on the radio. The theme was "to keep Nigeria one is a task that must be done." Although the ultimate aim of the war was successful in keeping Nigeria as one country, the impetus of the masses' demand for a better life resulted in the creation of more states. After the war, I went through primary school in the new Nigeria as we emerged from the civil war with the transitioning of military regimes.

At the village of Afowa, the Assumption Teachers Training College (for men) did not return to its main campus. It was rumored to have been relocated to a different location, far away. The unoccupied property created an opportunity for the missionaries to find alternative ways to make use of the abandoned campus. They did not waste time, and the vacant property was quickly converted into classrooms for a Catholic school for girls. It was the opportunity for St. Angela Girls Grammar School to be expanded from its location at the convent to the prime location closer to the church. Expatriate visitors, who were closely tied with the missionaries, stayed beyond the period of war but must have realized that the new Nigeria had embarked on a difficult journey of self-rule which would dwarf the influence of the missionaries in spreading Christianity.

Newly renovated Catholic church; picture taken December, 2017

Within a short window of opportunity, they introduced the idea of education for women. The government later followed with the introduction of compulsory primary education for all. The people at Afowa and within the Uzairue clan took a giant leap in benefitting from educating all their children ahead of many other places. Muslim, Christian, or non-religious females in my age group who completed elementary school had an opportunity to attend secondary school. It was a novel idea which was not widely popular in a society of decadence before the war. The rumors of degenerate immorality, of cannibalism, ritualistic killings, and armed robbery were reminders of the bottommost aspects of life among a people starved of the normal order of discipline and respect for order and human dignity during a military regime.

Aneke Cecilia

It was during the war that I began to spend a lot more time with my sister Aneke at the tutors' quarters where she lived with her family. At times I watched as the army trained and paraded. From there I went to visit my sister's house, and there, through the fence a distance from the main parade fields, I would continue to watch the army. I also spent some nights at my sister's place, a habit which my father disliked.

Baba had wanted our sister to attend school before she married, but once she was married, Baba expected her to raise her family with her husband and not be a burden to anyone. Although she started having children after she married, she retained her young-looking appearance. She always showed charisma with her charming smiles. The emblematic gap between her front teeth was wider than Peter's and mine, and her voice was soft. She had an excellent command of Afemai dialectic idioms. At 5 feet 8 inches, she was taller than Mama and she always wore pretty, multi-colored bubas and lapas, clean head ties, and slippers.

*Sister -Sibling Cecelia Aneke -
Always has a charming smile*

As I had always done and continued to do during the war, I often walked through the military camp area to visit my sister's house, where she and her family lived on a plot of land adjoining the military camp. When the military took over the college campus, they suspended the watchman. After they left, the watchman returned to his job. The area was guarded 24 hours a day, and the night watchman carried a long rifle called an *okodoh* (day gun). I sensed there were no bullets inside that gun but didn't want to mess with the watchman, nevertheless. Besides the watchman, I was also fearful of getting into trouble snooping around the campus, which basically consisted of avoiding encounters with the white people in the area.

Whether it was the white people—who were mostly reverend nuns or Catholic priests—I was careful whenever I was in the area around the mission. I did not understand or speak English at the time. The white people—especially the women—appeared to be whispering, unlike the African, open-mouth sound from the throat. Everyone seemed to be saying, "Yes, Sister," but I wasn't sure if they understood those whispering sounds or were just repeating the "yeses" to be polite.

In front of my sister's house, from a distance, I would watch the female students marching from the classrooms to the dormitories. Their dresses of bright blue and white presented an impressive sight. Whenever the white teachers were not around, one or two of the senior students would stop by to say few words or buy snacks. They referred to my sister as "Mama Cordelia," in the African, distinctive manner of politeness.

My sister always knew that I needed to be fed before I returned home after my visits. On one occasion she gave me groundnuts (peanuts). I nodded my thanks and went to the back of the house. I got the gari and poured water. Gari is like cereal when it was soaked in water, and it is eaten with other dishes like baked beans, okra, etc. As I sat on the bench and began to eat, one of the female students came to join me and shared my soaked gari.

She said, "Sister told me to join you."

I nodded in response.

I avoided any situation where I would have to speak English until my first year in high school. The most dreadful of these were the one-on-one encounters with oyibo—white people, the priests and reverend sisters—who were teachers at the area schools, but I did have a few unexpected meetings.

As I said, my sister's house was next to the girls school. When the school was in session, I always walked along the road to the end of the barbed-wire fence then cut across the girls school compound, which shortened my walk by five minutes. The shortcut posed the chance of getting caught by the watchman. Getting into an encounter with the watchman was serious enough; I did not even consider what to do if I found myself in the hands of the reverend sisters—nuns, as they are called in the United States. That did happen later on one of my walks.

The Biafra War changed our lives—in our village and throughout the entire nation. On a personal level, I did not return to the Demonstration School at Afowa. Although the elementary school reopened after the soldiers moved away, life was not the same as it had been. I did not think of school very much while it was closed, but I became more self-conscious that I did not have clothes to wear around the house.

Paul and Peter moved away from the village to resume schooling and Cecilia lived in the vicinity of the missionary quarters with her family, while Philip and I lived with our parents.

Later on, after the initial confusion had settled, the village took account of the young men who had joined the military. Out of our house, two of my nephews, who were about the same age as Paul, had joined the army once they completed Modern/Standard school—the equivalent of primary school—and made the military their career.

Preparations for Christmas, holidays, and other celebrations took on a special meaning for me because it was a time to indulge my fascination for new clothes. At Christmas I could expect new clothes or shoes, which I did not have at the time. I discussed my thoughts with Mother when the two of us were alone. "Mama," I said, "I would like have clothes for Christmas."

In her always unassuming manner, her response was, "I do not have the money to buy you clothes. The money I have I need to use to buy oil to cook our food. Go and ask your father to buy clothes for you."

Since mother did not have the money, my best chance would be to direct my request to my father. I had seen other children being taken to the tailor shop to be measured for dashikis, and I wanted him to do the same for me. But first I asked my brother Philip. "Philip," I said, "come, join me, let us go and ask Baba to buy Christmas clothes for us."

"I am not interested, you can go by yourself," he told me.

So I went to Baba and said, "Baba, I want to have new clothes for Christmas." I thought the matter settled, although Father did not say how he was going to get me the new outfit, whether or not he would give the money to Mama.

One evening Father called me and we walked over to Ikedu, the tailor. The shop was close to the mosque and village square. I was happy to see the pretty machines and rows of beautiful clothes. I smelled the sweet scent of the shop with its colorful displays of material used to sew dashikis and matching pants. I was entranced and pleased that my request to Baba had worked. "Happily, I will be getting sparkly new clothes for the first time in my life," I said.

At the shop, my father gave the traditional greeting of, "Moh, Eramha," to show he honored the village elders. I did not pay much attention as they spoke and my measurements were taken. My joy continued, knowing I was going to have new clothes.

For the first time, I will have long pants for Christmas, I kept reassuring myself. But, wait a minute. My heart sank, and I had the sneaking feeling "well maybe, maybe not" when I was not allowed to choose the material.

My disappointment was beyond painful when my new clothes turned out to be a khaki-nika—short pants—and a white, short-sleeved shirt. Other children had on their colorful outfits; I was one of the few who wore a only a khaki nika and white shirt that Christmas.

During the holiday season, there were celebrations where everyone—pagans, Muslims, Christians alike—celebrated something. The children would dress up in colorful outfits and would go from house to house, receiving gifts of money from the adults. I was so ashamed of attending the celebrations wearing my short pants and white shirt, especially since that year there was a ceremony, an initiation, at the large, village square for my older brother Paul's age group.

Paul was getting initiated into manhood, which by tradition was expected to be a lavish display of affluence celebrating that stage of life. Paul was over twenty years old and was supposed to be married. Most of the men in his age group were already married, and their wives and families provided support. The hype was more in the preparations for the carnival-style events, which took place over a period of three days, than the actual ceremony. At the village square, the initiates constructed tents from palm trees and wood. Each of the celebrants was assigned a spot in the makeshift tents which they decorated and displayed their treasures and ornaments. Musicians performed during the entire ceremony, while the initiates danced and celebrated with friends and family.

For various reasons I did not like Paul's manhood celebration. For one, I believed it was a waste of money. Years later, when my age group was initiated into manhood, my nephew stood in my place since I was already living overseas and could not be there for the ceremonies.

As I said earlier, I had become self-conscious about my appearance, and I was not happy that my new outfit was not fit for the celebrations. My nephew Emmanuel was dressed up, and I took him along with me to visit his aunt's house. Aunt Tina—they called her Itina—was always a pleasant person and very nice to me. Aunt Tina's husband, Arunah, seemed to have a lot money. During my visit to Aunt Tina's, I received money and gifts; I received more than anyone at the manhood celebrations.

After Christmas it became clearer to me that the khaki pants and white shirt were purposely made as my school uniform. The proof is in the memorable picture below that was taken of me in my uniforms.

David, in the back center: My first picture, ever, was taken at Cecilia's

Although Paul did not get married until later, after I completed secondary school, Baba had saved up for the dowry. It was regarded as one, if not the highest, obligation for the father to provide when the son married. I have had very wonderful experiences at wedding celebrations.

The dowry is part of the Nigerian culture and part of the traditional marriage celebration that has remained intact through the ages. Whether first, second, third, or fourth wife—like in my mother's case—the dowry was arranged and paid through negotiations with the bride's family. It was sacrosanct that the whole affair be handled with the utmost respect. The man's family brought kola nuts, palm wine, and money to ask for the "hand in marriage." The "proposal" was considered accepted when other family accepted those things.

On the special day, the man's family would come with the entire list of things as requested by the woman's family, accompanied by a band of musicians called *Izi*, the women's dance. One or two men usually played the talking drums, along with the women—at least five—who played the calabash gourd called the *aze*; which was the main instrument of the Izi. The shrill sounds of *aye-leh leh*, created from inside the deep throat with rapid repetitions welcomed the party.

"Aye-leh leh, aye-leh leh!" the women of the bride' family would squeal in excitement.

The party from the bridegroom's family would display the bevy of beautiful things they had brought, including bags of salt, rice, varieties of cooking oils—called *ololo*—hundreds or thousands of dried fish—bonga, catfish, etc.—and shiny silver and golden, colorful ornaments. There would be rounds and rounds of dancing and cheers would be exchanged.

After the dowry was settled, a date for the wedding would be set. That would be the date when the bride must leave her parents and unite with the husband and her new family. The dowry was not to be confused as selling the daughter. That was made clear throughout the back-and-forth negotiations. The girl's family would say, "We are not selling you our daughter for the price of the dowry. No amount of money can pay us for our daughter."

The wedding day became the crowning apex of merriment. It has since been modernized, but back in those days, the bride was treated as a virgin and was delivered to the husband as a "purity of virtue," meaning the bride was totally naked, but her body would be decorated with juice from the fruit of *abie* trees—the juice was a special, black color—and she would wear the prettiest head tie. She would be covered under the shade of a large, beautiful umbrella. The walk was dignified and deliberate, as women touted the bride's goodness along the way, accompanied by the sound of *apoghe*.

"Our daughter, she is good. She is the best! She does not have any bad manners. She does not steal. Our daughter does not spend time sneaking around. No one can accuse her of doing bad!" the women would call out.

Within the village of Afowa, the bride went through a final procession. They stopped at the village square, by which time she was completely surrounded by the crowd of women so that no one saw her nude body, only the head tie and the umbrella that shielded her. Often, in spontaneous solidarity, the girls and women around the bride would take off their dresses, purposely trying to steal attention from the beautiful bride.

The sound of a gun signaled the moment they arrived at the home of the new husband, and the Izi women dancers would be startled by the boom-bang noise of the smoking day gun. But the brave women quickly followed by echoing, "Aye-leh leh," in shrill voices to counter the men's noisy banging and the cloud of gun smoke saturating the air.

The Izi dance commenced as the "aye-leh leh" turned into a new tune and the tempo changed, and the women danced in a swirl around the bride. The group with the bride was ushered into the mother-in-law's quarters, where they gracefully knelt for her, and with open hands the mother-in-law took her new daughter amid tears and cheers of joy.

The bride would then be dressed in a native outfit of buba and lapa—the women's native blouse and matching clothe tied around the waist—and returned to be seated with the bridesmaids. The Izi dance continued into the night, and as the temperature cooled, there would be more dancing until the people began to request to see the newly married couple. Without much delay the newlyweds would be ushered onto the dance floor.

Chapter 3
St. Peters Central Primary School

My best friend at the time in elementary school was my cousin Bartholomew Afeakuna Idalu. We were neighbors and shared one big compound. By the time we were in the third year, our school schedule was changed from a half day—for years one and two pupils—to a full day. Other relatives in my class were Catherine Idalu (Babi) and Osioakpeme Uloko. All three were older and bigger than me. I was shy and somehow intimidated by the other students who were not from my village.

Afeakuna was a few years older but the same age as my brother Philip. He was active in school activities, attended church in the morning, and joined the school band. He carried the drums for the bigger boys and moved up to being a drummer boy by the end of his second year.

One school day Afeakuna took the lead and a few of our classmates went to his father's (Idalu) cocoa farm—in the garden at the village—to pick fresh beans. Ripe coffee beans were highly desirable, but the trees planted at school were not allowed to have fully matured beans. After school hours the schoolyard was an attractive place for some stubborn, fearless pupils who were drawn like magnets to watch for fruit that fell from the trees.

On this day, by the time we returned to the school after our visit to the cocoa farm, recess was over. I vowed not to partake in such truancy again. On the few times we were caught, we would receive lashes. Whether or not it was the fear of corporal punishment and the shame of being caned, we would quickly change our behaviors, but corporal discipline remained widely accepted. The parents expected the child to be flogged at school for disobeying people at home. Everyone was afraid of the teachers, often to a much larger extent than the parents.

"I am not going to wait around the house in the mornings to wake you up for school," my mother said.

"Mama," I pleaded. "Please, I beg you, wake me up in morning."

She responded, saying, "I am doing more than enough already. I cook the soup, so do not expect me to take care of you like a baby before you go to school. You're old enough for school. The teacher will be waiting for you if you are late."

"But, Mama, all I ask is that you wake me up. I will take care of myself."

She wasn't swayed by my pleas. I had to face the challenges squarely.

Philip attended Demonstration School, but he began to skip school in the third year. Mama caught up with Philip for disobeying and went after him with the broom. With the broom raised high, she landed it from his waist area to his thighs. Philip screamed to get attention, even if he was not getting struck hard, since Mama was talking. "Didn't I tell you not to do that? Go and kneel down over there."

Philip ran away from the kitchen, and Mama seemed to regret the beating, as the broom left some marks on Philip's light-yellow complexion.

I was scared. Mama had never beaten us with the broom before, so I hoped that it was not going to be me the next time. I saw that Mama was very angry because her words were not getting across to Philip.

Mama said, "I can't chase you around. You make me ashamed." Philip had run off and couldn't hear her, but she called out, "You will receive the same kind of treatment you gave me. I will not curse you. I do not curse at my children, but you only curse is for you to have children. Your children will give you back double the trouble you have given me."

I felt the sting of those words, especially when I did something to upset her. She would call me that nasty name of *obie egbe bie agu,* meaning "black in the body and black in the mind."

It was a terrible thing to be called, because I knew how black our steel cooking pot was, and it was beyond imagining that my insides and heart would be so black. It was definitely a curse to worry about. Showing a little bit of gratitude would change Mama's heart, so I behaved better to her keep happy and after that she called me the bad names less and less. Most of the time she called the name of praise, "*Adebidi, Asa-mali, Oghie luku-luku, Oghieneni, Odala-ubile…..*"

The irony of those impressionable years, as it turned out, was that the caning may have caused emotional trauma and encouraged school drop-out. Yet school was preferable to many of us than going to the farm, which was exactly what the parents used to scare us with. "Go to school or go to the farm with us," they would say. Somehow, Philip was able to avoid school and also stay away from the farm.

The push broom sweeping the compound sounded like the "swish-swishing of the washing machine," and the rhythm of mother's hymns "*Aigbo ni yosimhe ki yale*" meaning, "Life, I told my Lord, will be good for me. Lord, deliver me from all temptations, and do not let me fall so that the enemy will laugh at me."

"Wake up, Philip! Wake up! Let's get ready for school. We are going to be late."

There was no response as I dozed and fell back to sleep. The sunlight penetrated through the window like a beam of light on the wooden bed where we slept in the room we shared with Baba. The beam of light signaled me that it was time to get up if I wanted to avoid being late—which was always at the back of my mind.

At times the noise would prompt me to get up, as I realized that I could not blame Philip anymore. I would make haste to Mama's kitchen, get the fire going, and boil a pot of water, followed with a scoop of gari in the pot to make the eba. The pot of soup went on the fireplace to be warned for a few minutes while I washed my face, arms, and legs. I would hastily eat the eba I prepared and then head out of the house. I had to remember my responsibility to pick up my school box as I headed for school. During those early years of elementary school, the constant worries of being late and getting caned might have helped me to shape up.

As with the morning routine at home, there were many rules to follow at school. Ms. Ekhelar and Mr. Emaleh—Papa—taught the rules and some of the dos and don'ts. We learned quickly to avoid getting teased and laughed at when we vomited. My teachers taught, "It is good to avoid eating cold food for breakfast." (Of course, eba—in varying forms—was my breakfast.) "Cold soup," they said—which was usually the cold *ogbono*—"causes you to get sick."

The teachers made a song in our dialect to remind the students about eating warm food:

"We are going to be dismissed from school.

I will eat eba and warm soup at home

And return to school right after the short break—

Teacher, the one who taught us books."

There were many scary things throughout the village—such as the voodoos and burial grounds—once I left the comfort of our house. The walk to school took me halfway through the village and then the footpath branched off by the old adult school building. The wooded path was a shortcut, but it was scary, which deterred me from walking there alone. The area was a burial ground for dead babies. Some areas around the footpath were filled with animal sacrifices (*izobos*). The alternate route was to walk on the main street and through the missionary quarters at the Catholic church. Although it was less scary to go through the church area, it meant being late to school. Whenever I missed the other kids, I ended up on the longer road through the church, often arriving late at school.

Gregory Idodo—my brother-in-law—was the headmaster (called HM by his teachers). Gregory was replaced by his younger brother Lawrence Idodo when Gregory left to pursue further studies at a teachers training college. Lawrence was stricter with the cane and showed a meaner side while at school, so I avoided contact with him. I shied away from my in-laws once I realized they were the ones in charge of my school, but I remained close to my sister and family.

Mrs. Ekhelar—Mamy Pauli—became my teacher in primary one after Joka departed within the first few weeks. The teacher for primary two was Mr. Emaleh, who was old and came out of retirement to teach. At the beginning of my third year, I missed many days, almost a month's time between January and February. Many things and changes happened in primary three, but the same teachers would be interchanged for the classes, so I had the experience of getting taught by the friends of my sister and her husband. Although some of my close relatives taught in the school system, I never had any of them as my teacher.

After the holidays, at beginning of the third year of school, a new delicacy of roasted cashew seeds became popular among the school children in the village. We had always consumed the delicious juice made from fresh cashews. We had plenty of cashew trees, since one of my brothers, the school teacher—*Iticha*—Boniface Akhalumhe, had planted many trees at the garden of Okotogba.

Parents issued warnings that eating cashew seeds could kill us, but the warnings did not stop us, since the crunchy, sweet, roasted cashews were irresistible. We figured out how to roast cashew seeds in makeshift fires using a canister which safely let the cashew's acidic skin burn away. This was crucial. We were careful after roasting the seeds to wait a little bit for everything to cool off before cracking the shells to release the roasted cashews.

One day in January, which was the beginning of the school year of primary three, Bartholomew Afeakuna Idalu, my close friend, Fede (Fedilis) Ogbhemhe, and I had collected cashew seeds and we gathered at my mother's kitchen, which was in a secluded area away from the two big compounds. I was the youngest among us three, and we went on with roasting cashew nuts, despite the warning that eating cashew nuts could kill us. The roasted delicacy presented an irresistible urge.

Afeakuna said, "You have another person with you. I thought we agreed it would be just the two of us."

I responded, "Fede picked some of the cashew seeds, so we have to roast together and then we can share."

"Are you sure that he will not tell on us?" Afeakuna asked. Then he said, "Here, bring the stone over here so I can make holes in the bottom of the can. Fede! Hold onto the can like this!"

I stood and watched as the two made a few holes.

"Go and make the fire," Afeakuna told me.

"The last time I did the roasting with you and Philip, we were in back of the house. We buried the can. Why do you want to roast right here in Mama's kitchen?" I asked.

"Go and get the fire. We'll be done before anyone returns home."

I ran over to the other part of the house and fetched the burning fire and got our fire going. We placed the nuts in the can and allowed them to roast, as the fire seemed to burn off the juices. The nut began to darken as it was turned over with a long stick until the roasting was completed. The can was emptied of its contents and left sitting idly nearby. None of us paid any mind to the hot can.

"Hey! We have to crack all the nuts first and then we can share."

Afeakuna was good, suggesting what we had already agreed upon. I suspected they had a plan to trick me and run off, so I remained vigilant, keeping a close watch on the cashews.

We took turns selecting the nuts we wanted. The whole cashews got picked first and then only halves and tiny pieces were left. I quickly ate my share, knowing that we had to get rid of the evidence. However, we started shoving to get the remaining pieces. I was pushed and I lost my balance, falling onto the kitchen floor. The sharp pain in the side of my belly made me scream! "Ouch! Ouch …"

The boys continued struggling, unaware that I was hurt. The hot canister burned a nasty hole on the side of my belly. There were no adults around. I guess the screams must have caught the attention of my older niece, Ikpaluobe—in Afemai dialect the name means "I am not the first in sin." She came and took control of the situation after my friends panicked and ran.

Ikpaluobe applied Shea butter to the open wound. "David, be careful, do not move. You'll be fine. Here, lay down on the mat." As in the meaning of her name, she had a "kind heart" and was not the first to do evil. She placed a mat on the floor, where I lay and fell asleep.

The incident with the hot canister became the talk everywhere throughout the surrounding villages and served as a warning for school kids about the danger of eating cashew nuts. I heard stories about the boy who was burned. I stayed out of school while I recovered and received treatment for the burn at the dispensary. News gets so distorted. It may be unintentional, but rumors were the way information got around to warn us about doing things we were not supposed to do. Notwithstanding the adults' monitoring, we were quick to create ways to keep busy.

On the last day of school, we were handed our report cards to take home. Every pupil received a report card and knew exactly which position they were placed in class. Under the shade of the huge Ogi tree, the pupils in primary one and two were assembled in a circle.

The teacher called out each student by name. The first student called was the best in the class because he or she took the 1st place:

"Killian, first place." And everyone clapped and cheered.

Second and third places were announced, and those students were given their report cards as they exited the circle to the cheers of their older siblings. I was almost at the point of losing my composure when I heard the teacher call, "David Akhamie." It was great since I was the only David in class. Yes! Yes!

For me, it was like I had taken first in class, although I was disappointed that I had not actually done so. However, I was relieved that I had passed and that I was among the top ten in my class. I exited the circle.

Further down the line, to about the twentieth place, one or two pupils were informed they had "failed" and would have to repeat the class.

When I got home I was very happy to inform Mama, "I passed! I was promoted to primary two."

"Wonderful!" Mama said as she nurtured me with praises to celebrate my promotion.

Chapter 4

Caning, Discipline, and Lessons

Arriving late to assembly meant the pupils were locked out and would have to kneel down by the gate to wait for the head master. The unfortunate ones who were kneeling would endure a caning before going to class and might be unlucky enough to miss their teachers' homework review. Boys were beaten on the buttocks and girls were beaten on the palms of open hands.

Was I scared of the cane? Heck, yes, I was. I did not want to be punished by such beatings. In order to avoid the cane, I stayed out of trouble—with the exception of unavoidable squabbles. But there was the unforgettable incident between me and Mr. Sunday Ayemoba, who taught the primary six students. During recess one day, as I was playing outside in the school yard, one of the pupils from another class instigated a quarrel by asking, "What do you have in your hand?"

Before I could muster any words, the boy and his friends accused me and pointed at the pictured I had sketched out of boredom during class. Not understanding, I replied, "What!"

Shy, surprised, and shunned by their accusations, I didn't know how to react. I thought maybe I had been naughty to sketch with an ink pen. In primary one, we used white chalk. Maybe we were not supposed to handle pens and pencils, and it was perceived as bad behavior.

"You're in trouble. We are going to report you to the teacher," the tattletales warned me as they ran towards Mr. Ayemoba. They handed over the piece of paper as I trembled in trepidation, wondering what I had done. The boys returned with a message, like a summons, that, "The teacher wants you to come." Walking between the two of them felt like I was in an escort hold; I couldn't melt away and disappear.

Mr. Ayemoba; the strict canner, got me. He dismissed the others. "Go back to your classroom," he told them. "David, come with me"

I wondered whether I was going to receive lashes. By far, he was one of the strictest teachers in the whole school. Whenever he ordered, "Carry him!," it meant the boy would be carried on the back of another, bigger boy and held tight in such a way as to immobilize the victim. Mr. Ayemoba would raise the dried stick cane and administer the lashes. As onlookers, we counted along as he handled the cane. "Six lashes, my friend," he would announce loudly.

He caned, and we recited, "One, two, three, four, five, six." The big boys just took those strokes on the buttocks without a sniffle or moan.

As I knelt in his classroom, Mr. Ayemoba did not have the bigger students hold me. I waited in anticipation for my punishment, but the cane did not land on me. Mr. Ayemoba displayed the image of the "thing" I sketched. Some laughed and called me a nasty boy. Others did not say anything; they didn't even make eye contact with me.

I missed recess and stayed in Mr. Ayemoba's classroom while he taught until the primary one and primary two pupils were dismissed. All my classmates had left; still I waited until school closed, worried and scared that I would have to walk home alone.

Mr. Ayemoba had a houseboy named Sunday who was, by coincidence, also his student. Sunday witnessed the entire episode of how I was embarrassed by his master. "Don't worry," he assured me. "You will be fine!" The young Sunday was handsome, tall, fair skinned, and a very nice person. We were neighbors and I had witnessed on several occasions when he was beaten by Mr. Ayemoba.

After the incident with me and the drawing, Mr. Ayemoba left home to pursue further education. However, the depravity of his personality continued, as the esteemed yet naughty professor beat his wives and carried on the demeaning, violent treatment of women. In an era of allegiance to the traditional, and focus on family, the men dominated their wives and got away with many things because of their educational status. I have often wondered what became of Sunday, the houseboy, who left school after he completed primary six. "Does he remember the caning and wife beatings?" I wonder.

The so-called discipline for the sake of good behavior was entrusted to teachers to take care of the boys and girls, for better or for worse. Serious matters such as sexual assaults and child abuse were scarce, but when they did occur, they were often deflected by placing the blame on no one, not the teacher and not on the students, who had been forewarned, as in the song that said:

Come to my house. The Iticha (teacher) said, Come!

Where do you want me to walk? the student asked.

Ok, walk in the center of the door.

What if the door does not let me?

Sneak through the window.

What if the window does not allow me?

Iticha said, "Go back home."

I hated the ugly act of caning in the elementary school but also had many pleasant memories of most of my class teachers. It was a memorable period when some of Afowa's teachers were assigned to my school: Mr. Francis Elogie—aka Hamahgha—was one of those interesting teachers who returned to the village to complete his tenure before he retired. Also very nice and pleasant teachers were Mr. Oboste and his wife, who returned home to the village and taught at the primary school. Even better for me was to have their first son, Festus Oboste, who was about my age, attend the same elementary school. Mr. Elogie was a hefty man and had a big, resounding, deep voice. "I am going to cane you hard, like the hammer, hamahgha," he would say.

He usually threatened to use the cane as the "hamahgha," so the pupils nicknamed him Mr. Hamahgha. But in reality he was not a mean person, so I was not afraid of him.

Like Hamahgha, some of the teachers received nicknames for being outright strict and rigid, like the old colonial masters. They were stuck in the old era when teachers were regarded as the "elites" and honorable, so we nicknamed the female teachers "Ticha" or "Miss." By the time I reached primary six in elementary school, the notorious teacher nicknamed Mr. "Deti"—which means dirty—had mellowed somewhat and treated me nicely. I found most of the teachers were intelligent in their steadfast passion to mold our lives for the better and to prepare us for a future of learning. Such a person was Mr. Elogie, who introduced the marching song:

Don't you know that?

We are Uzairue scholars.

We are Uzairue pupils.

Don't you know that?

We are Uzairue scholars.

If you want to know-ooh us,

Come to Central School!

Before long the song caught fire within the village and for a while it was like the anthem, and it certainly reigned number one for the marching band for a long time.

The Favorite Teacher

Mr. Emaleh was a retired teacher who taught primaries one and two and was known to many as Papa. An elderly man, he always carried snuff, which he pinched with his thumb and then sniffed inside his nose, one nostril at a time. Then he would blow his the nose, covered with a handkerchief, before he returned to teaching. We all regarded him to be the least strict since he did not use the cane on us. He was our favorite teacher, and everyone was lucky to have him. He had the slight accent of the Agenebode clan. Mr. Emaleh used folktales to introduce us to literature with stories of the monster Ogobolo and the brilliant tortoise called *egi*.

We loved the periods for social studies, vernacular, and oral literature, which were conducted in a more relaxed setting than the rigorous academic work. Those easy periods took place after our recess, and the teacher would take the stage to dramatize Afemai literature. Many pupils were shy and did not know many stories which would fit within the structured lesson period. I knew many stories which I could have altered to suit the purpose, but I held back because of occasional shyness to take the stand. Throughout the year the teachers labored to try to find pupils who could rev up the class with exciting stories. The students were often unable to meet the challenge. To avoid repeating the same stories, one day classes A and B were combined for the period, and Mr. Emaleh told stories of the monster—*Ogobolo-Agenebode/Uvgbaaleh-Uzairue*, the smart he-goat—*uyuko*, and the tiger, *ekpe*.

Thomas, a student nicknamed Atigo, was called upon to tell a story. He began his story according to the customary call to attention:

"*Okahi meh na riiheee ra du bgeh eghie*. This is the story about the tortoise," and he went on and on for long time, ever ending it.

The teacher assured us we would continue the story the next week. I admired Atigo on the way home from school, since I was impressed that he took the stand and was undaunted in the effort. However, the next week, Atigo continued with his stories, on and on, without ending.

Halfway through literature period, Ms. Ekhelar stopped him and asked, "Where are we going with the stories? There is no answer, no beginning, and no end." The teacher called for dismissal, and we joined the assembly at the end of the day. Thereafter, a term was created for the students who would tell stories without meaning: "*ee formu formu,*" meaning hogwash or gibberish. Shyness was no concern of Atigo, so whenever he took the stand for more than a few minutes, it was appropriate for us to call, "ee formu formu." A few students began to venture forth and take the stand, but none were able to dethrone our teacher and storyteller, Mr. Emaleh.

I envied Papa Emaleh as the king of Afemai folktales but eschewed calling, "ee formu formu"—that would be bad manners—and I continued to practice my act in case of a chance for me to take the stand. In the meantime, I listened with keen interest to Mr. Papa's stories, especially the one about the goat and the tiger. The story depicted the billy goat as a smart, domestic animal who won a contest against the tiger. In all sincerity, I thought it was out of character for goat to chase away a tiger.

My friend Atigo had lost out on his bid to be the class storyteller, but the teacher continued to ask for volunteers. One day I raised my hand.

"David, stand up and tell us your story," the teacher said.

Without making eye contact, and gazing at my forefinger, I started, "Okahi meh na rii ra du bgeh…" (i.e., Once upon a time, there was a jealous woman …" The class listened as my voice rang out and they sang along.

The story was short and included a song with a happy ending about a treasure of gold and silver. The total silence in the room allowed my shy voice to convey a feeling of confidence. At the end the teacher clapped and my classmates joined in the ovation. My face shone happily, and my relief was evidenced by my full smiles. I knew that was the one day I made an impression by telling my stories of Afemai.

Lessons of Oral History

In grade school, our culture was told through oral history, so we went on many field trips to the neighboring villages of Afashio, Afowa, and Jattu. Since my school was located at the center of the three villages, it was easy to visit any of them during school trips.

It was during my absence from school that my class went on an excursion to Afashio, and when they started the lessons on Uzairue's history, Ms. Elamah told the students to be nice to me and to help out with regards to the material that I had missed. Worse was the social studies taught during my absence: the beginning of the history of Uzairue. At Afashio my class explored the mysteries of Inekeze, which was about the sword of magic that usually appeared during the rainy seasons. Some of my classmates from Afashio talked about the trip. "I have seen the sword before after a heavy rain," Olayinka confided in me.

"Do you think you can show me the spot?" I asked my friend.

"Yes, it was over there around the footpath in the place called Inekeze. The ticha said that was the place where the migrants from Bini made their tents."

I was happy that Olayinka was able to fill me in on the lessons I had missed, especially the information about Afashio. I was able to rely on my natural curiosity to learn more about the history of the Uzairue clan.

Afowa had its shrines in the village squares; there was a small one and another one at the bigger village square on the road to Elele. The footpath leading to Elele, which is the village to the north side of Afowa, used to be the residing place of another shrine, but the main shine was the portion of land and the cottage at the village main square called the utukue. The shrine was regarded as sacred. No one messed with it.

Occasionally the priest—who was usually a male designated by the royal family—performed rituals. The men and elders always gathered at the native wood benches located next to the shrine at Utukue. They maintained guard over the village.

One day during recess, Olayinka took me to Afashio. We stopped at Olayinka's house, where we met with his mother, a Yoruba woman. Both his parents were Yorubas and had settled at Afashio to raise a family.

"I was not able to eat before I left home. So I want to eat before we go to Afashio," Olayinka said. He walked inside the house and said few words with his mother, who peeked out of the room as if to see who I was.

"Moh, Mama," I greeted her.

She answered me but relied on Olayinka to translate, since she did not speak Afemai. But she seemed to be more preoccupied with her daughter, who wanted to play with Olayinka. Moments later the father walked by where I was waiting, and we gestured an exchange of greetings as he walked away towards their assembly place for the men.

Olayinka joined me after he finished eating eba with ogbono soup, and we headed out towards the Inekeze shrine. "I made a promise that I was going to show you around Afashio. Our first stop will be at the shrine. You have to be quiet and must not point at the place unless you want the shrine to strike you," he explained.

Olayinka and I started primary one the same year but had not always been in the same class. He was regarded as a troublemaker because he fought often and was not afraid of the teachers and the cane. Others feared and almost avoided him, especially when he was in the company of Batoto and his brother Albert. Unlike the bad brothers, who skipped classes to go hunting for 'possums and rats with their dogs, Olayinka was nice to be with when his friends were not around. Fortunately, they were out of school that day, so Olayinka and I were able to perambulate the village, but I still had a keen sense of caution.

We passed through the shrine as quiet as church mice and went to the giant cherry (*ochie*) tree. It was school hours, but many were there during recess. We walked to the south side of the village along the footpath to the village of Idato and sat under the shade of the cherry tree, which was smaller than those giant trees Olayinka climbed to pluck the cherry fruit.

"I did not know you could climb this big tree! How do you know how to do so many things?" I asked.

"I was not born at Afashio, but my parents brought me here as a child. I have lived here most of my life."

"Do you know whether you will return to the place where your father came from?"

He simply shook his head and said, "I do not worry, my home is Afashio."

As we walked back to school, Olayinka told me a story about the Uzairue that he remembered from class, and I reflected on what had I missed during my absence.

"The Uzairue clan was made up of various villages founded by families who migrated from Bini," Olayinka told me. "One of the leaders was a man called Ikpe, and he was accompanied by other families that had decided to separate from of the Bini kingdom. They did not like the taxation policies and limited freedom. There were too many rules and constant interferences from the *Oba*.

"Ikpe left with his whole family, which was comprised of his sons, Ashio, Ovwa, Eke, and others. They settled at present-day Jattu, which is still the seat of the clan's leader, "the Oghieneni of Uzairue." From there the children went to farm in the surrounding area, which became their land settlements.

"Eke, the oldest son, travelled farther away towards the northeast and settled in that area with his family. At first the family went to work at the farm, which they called Imeke—meaning the farm of Eke. Over the years, it grew into the settlement village of present-day Imeke. Similar situations took place with the younger brothers, Ashio and Ovwa. The parents, who had stayed at their original settlement and founded Ikpe, went to visit their relatives. 'We are going to our family—afe—of Ashio,' they said. As the years went by, they founded the village of Afashio. The relatives would say, 'We are going to our family at Ovwa,' and that formed the name of Afowa."

This was the lesson learned in elementary school history. That despite the rancor of ethnicity and the Biafra War, we—at Afashio and Afowa—were founded by siblings.

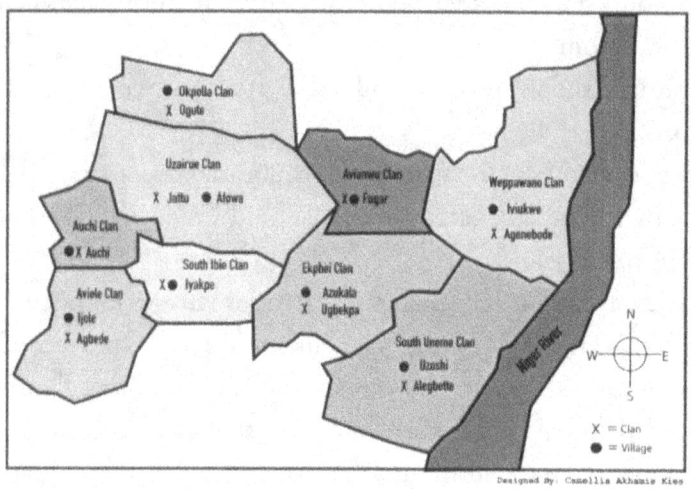

Estako Division, Bendel State

Missionary School Compounds

The Catholic missionary owned the schools, but the Teachers Training Demonstration School was assumed to be the Afowa village primary school. One year while I was attending the school, there was a teacher—nicknamed Alleh—from Afowa, who took upon himself the task of protecting the school from vandals. In that year the mango fruit was left alone until the fruit was ripe. Word got around that anyone caught vandalizing the school and the mangoes would be flogged severely. The headmaster was Mr. Okpaloafe—meaning, "the one in front for the family"—who also happened to be my in-law through marriage to my niece. My brother Peter was the senior monitor in primary six, and Peter ensured that any students who violated the rules were reported to the teachers. The mango trees survived for many years before eventually succumbing to the ill fate of neglect and death.

The school had to be swept clean with coconut or palm brooms every morning before school started. Some of the students swept and cleaned, while others were assigned various leadership positions to monitor different tasks. These duties were taken seriously, and the senior boys made sure pupils assumed their responsibilities. A position carried influence beyond the school yard, even to the students' homes.

The village schools were comprised of mostly boys, since girls did not go very far beyond a few years of elementary school. The Demonstration School served as the practical training site for students who went on to attend Assumption Teachers Training College. From the main entrance gate of Demonstration School, a side entrance was available for the college students to enter the primary school.

A few yards farther along was the compound of the Catholic missionaries, which had various social activities. As such, the centralized location seemed to be well situated for schools, church, tutors' quarters, and the cemetery.

Drum beats, along with marching songs, prepared children for the beginning of each daily instruction. St. Peters was located close to the cemetery and the giant Catholic church, but the close proximity to the cemetery gave me a weird feeling; I didn't care to be so close to the graveyard. Worse yet, there was the ever-smelling latrines located at the edge of the cemetery. I dreaded using the latrines and would rather return home to go in the large expanse of wooded area around my home. Peeing was not a problem for the boys; it was just a matter of going to a secluded area. I avoided using the latrine at school and only went in the woods at home.

I have great memories of various activities during school or holidays, especially during the Catholic Harvest Thanksgiving, Christmas, Easter, or New Year's. Occasionally, the students had songs denigrating the prestige of an opposing school, and at times there were physical confrontations between students during sports activities. The Demonstration School was a newer school, built to accommodate children who were of school age from the villages within walking distance of the Catholic mission. It later turned into a place of pride for Afowa.

By our fifth year, it was announced that officials were looking for students to attend the seminary. Barth applied and was selected. He would have to travel to Benin City, away from home, and stay at the hostel for secondary school. Such a great move served as an awakening that my classmate—although Barth was older, the same age as Phillip, we had spent the previous four years together—would now be in high school. He showed courage, a giant step of ambition in a positive direction.

"Everyone has a moment in life. Your moment will come." Mama listened and talked about the seemingly "minute of things," as the men would say. Such advice aided me and I forged ahead. Barth and I exchanged letters about his life at Benin City for the few years, but we drifted apart after I went to grammar school.

Barth was known for his native name of Afeakuna—meaning "the profound symbol of family." We could have nicknamed him Afe—meaning "family" in Afemai—but it was fashionable to be westernized as a "guy" or "cool." We shared the same position as the last born of our families. He had grown brothers and sisters who had their own children. Both he and I were uncles to some older family members, and we also shared the circumstances of our older siblings being our keepers, those responsible for us at home. We both shared resentful feelings of having to report to our senior siblings.

"David, I have will have to receive confirmation because I am a servant at mass. My baptismal name is Bartholomew." That was about the time I started calling him Barth, since the native name Afeakuna seemed odd at the time

"I wonder how you can understand what the *Fada*—the Roman Catholic priests—say, since you do not speak English. I have not been baptized yet. Was it difficult for you to be baptized?" I asked hm.

"No, you will have to learn the catechism and pass the test. The test is given by the Fada to make sure you know how to be a Christian."

"But the Fada does not speak our tongue. How does he know you are not just making gibberish?" I asked.

Many of our friends had already been baptized to receive Holy Communion. The gap between me and my mate was getting wider and I was missing out.

"I will attend extra classes at the church, where they are giving evening classes to prepare for the test," I told him. Then I said, "Hey, Barth, do I have to get a new name since my name is David?"

"No, but I will be your sponsor and you will have to give them your date of birth." he said.

"I do not know my date of birth. How did you get your date of birth?" I asked.

"It is OK. Just pick one date in the same year that most of your mates were born."

The training and excitement over baptism seemed to have encouraged us to make so many promises that not too many of us could keep in complying with the Ten Commandments.

"David, you must swallow the whole communion at once, right there at the altar."

"Is that why it is called the body of Christ? I heard that it would turn to blood if anyone takes the communion out of the church."

"No, I have not experienced any incident with the blood, but there was the story of a man who took the communion home to show his wife. The whole thing was a mess, and the Fada had to say mass."

"How can one avoid getting into trouble?" I asked.

"You must take confession with the Fada once every week before you walk up the aisle and kneel at the altar to receive communion."

"Hey, Barth, I really learn a lot from you, but what about looking at girls? Is it a sin? We have always talked about the girls we like."

"You have to confess to Fada, which is all I know!"

Barth's assertive nature pushed him but also came with trouble for us, so I had to be more careful for my own sake, which eventually paid off for me, as I became the class monitor during my fourth year. The teachers sometimes selected the top students to be the class monitors. The monitor performed the duties assigned by the teacher and reported misbehaving students. He would be flogged and removed from his position if he misbehaved.

Between Barth and me, our ultimate test came during examination month. The class examination papers were folded in a roll, tied with a knotted string, and given to me to take home. Barth also had his classmates' examination papers. After school on the way home, Barth bragged to the other students that we both had our classmates' examination papers. The students asked us to show then the grades for our class. They tried to convince me. I thought it was the wrong thing to do.

"You cannot continue to say no!" Barth said as he joined the others to pressure me to show the grades. "You are too scared," he said.

I knew it was trouble but could not escape the teasing of my schoolmates. Upon my arrival at home, I neatly unfolded the papers, read them over, and tied them up again. I was happy: I had done well. Later that evening Barth came over to my house, and we opened up the students' papers to compare grades.

Barth's brother-in-law, Mr. Momodu of Jattu, was his class teacher, while Mr. Ekundayo, his friend, was mine. "You looked at the class exam papers?" Mr. Ekundayo asked me.

"No, sir."

"Go back to your seat!"

The situation did not go quite so well with my friend. Right after the morning assembly, I could sense something awful was about to happen because Afeakuna (Barth) was taken outside his classroom by his teacher to be questioned.

Afeakuna had told the others, who had gone to the teachers. From where I was in my classroom, I saw Afeakuna getting lashed by his teacher. It was painful to have one's brother-in-law as the classroom teacher. I was fortunate my brother-in-law did not cane as much for the short time he was my school's headmaster.

The good sides of the in-law relationship outweighed the caning, since we used the time after school to visit our sisters. It was even better when we visited Jattu, where Afeakuna's sister—called Omoitse—lived with her husband, the teacher Mr. Momodu of Jattu. The mother-in-law—Mama Walter—at Jattu operated a restaurant (buka). We continued to make regular trips after Omoitse went to the city with her husband. The attraction was the mother's cooked rice and stew, and she made sure we were fed every time we came to visit.

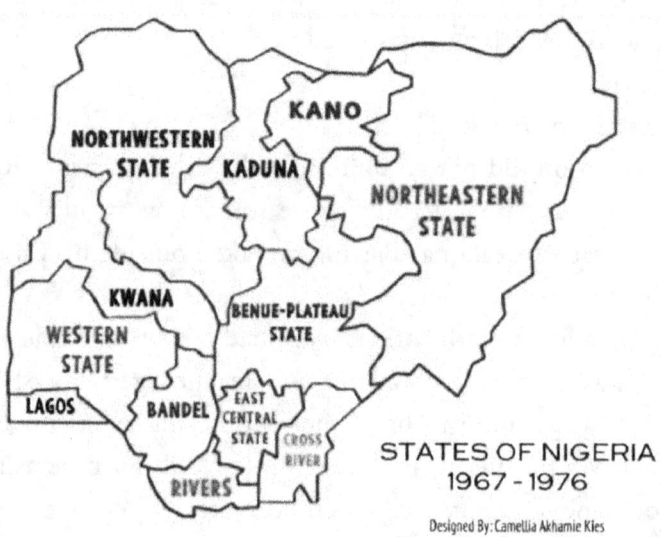

STATES OF NIGERIA 1967 - 1976

Designed By: Camellia Akhamie Kies

Chapter 5

Afe ("Family")

The elders held steady to the belief of *afe*—family—being the root and strength of a people. A person without a family was seen as one who was isolated with no person around, in front of, behind, or to the left or right. Each person had a certain purpose for the family and that has remained the core part of my life.

The celebration of birth was something bigger, in the fashion of the traditional celebration of Esi, a festival of thanksgiving, and others events to commemorate ancestors or the one who made things possible, which is God. The names of the children resonate the belief that an ancestor is responsible for bringing babies—such names as Etu or Ogu. Paul was called Ogu, which he disliked but which was accepted practice for males born at the time. It was believed that they were incarnated through the ancestral Ogu. Aneke—meaning the "princess," named after Inene—was the nickname of my sister Cecilia. Such tradition has been replaced by naming children after parents, aunts, uncles, godfathers or mother since Christianity has replaced long-held traditional beliefs.

As head of the family, Baba didn't believe in unknown ancestral spirits like Ogu, so he gave native Afemai names to each of us. Each birth, time, and season was an opening for him to recount his family's story. Such was the case with Agbasovhelo—Agbaso, "life is good"; Osikhemekhai—"God gives me greatness"; Imiegomhe—"I receive my gold"—and all my other brothers and sisters. I have had the solemn experience of witnessing my father at the naming of the each newborn.

Naming Ceremony

When a child was born in our household, Imaatu, the third wife, served as the matron. She cared for and bathed the baby, using special herbs cooked in boiling water. Every morning she sat on the stool called *Ighoko*, and the newborn was treated to a warm bath. She pressed the baby firmly on her lap, turned face down to massage the back area, face up to massage the stomach and around the umbilical cord and head. As the baby cried with eyes tightly closed, she exercised the baby's limbs from the tips of the toes to the fingers, and with both hands threw the baby up in the air:

We counted at each throw, "*U Whey u-wey; u whey u-wey,* and up to about five throws. Then the bath was done and the baby was handed over to the mother.

The new mother received special care, eating a special soup made with real hot peppers and alligator peppers as the main ingredient. At times I have been enticed by my sister to eat some of the new-mother's soup. It was nothing that I would try again. The soup was pepper hot.

Usually, after seven days, the new mother prepared a dish of pounded yam and *egusi* as an offering to the ancestors. Baba held the baby and entered his room and stood in front of the *Etu* shrine. He called on his father, Osigwe, and the past generations to thank them, and he gave the evocation, "Protect the baby which you have given to our family with a long and prosperous life."

Upon returning the baby to the mother, he announced the baby's native name to the mother. Every child had a native name, which became the middle name in the new era of Western influence.

TITLES OF BABA AND UNCLE

It was an honorable thing for Baba to follow the custom of recounting episodes and great deeds of his Baba to his offspring, such as the notable praises for the child of Akhamiemona, tailor, shoemaker, basket weaver, farmer, trader, and investor. Recounting deeds of the departed ensured the legacy was not forgotten, and the retelling bolstered and motivated the next generations to carry on the legacy.

Grown children mentioned the names of their departed parents and grandparents, which was a show of respect of their life achievements. Using the name of Osigwe when speaking of my grandfather showed that I knew my ancestors.

It was during my visit to the village in 2005, when I met Uncle Sunday Dekeri, mother's younger brother from Okpella, that Baba passed. As the only uncle, he carried on Baba's position of honor. He used the occasion to bring me and my siblings together for pep talks. "I modeled my own life after that of Baba," he told us.

Uncle Sunday went on to reiterate his story as the last child and only son of his mother. "I did not have anyone to train me. I did not go to school."

Without a formal education, nevertheless, he made a prosperous life as a businessman. "*Na Baba na hem mi dey luk fo bisnes,*" said in pidgin. That meant that it was through Baba that he knew about business ideas. However, life had turned better for Uncle Sunday and extended to his son, my cousin Anamero Dekeri, who had become a successful entrepreneur and operated several companies, including Dekeri Nigerian Ltd., the Danco Group, Gulf Treasures, and other concerns in Nigeria.

Sunday Dekeri (Uncle) and wives
Sunday Dekeri is from Okpella. As a young man, he grew up without anyone to send him to school and provide a formal education. Through his own ingenuity he became an entrepreneur and started business of dealing in local cash produce like palm kernel and cocoa along with his farming. Mr. Dekeri passed on the knack of business to his children out of which emerged my nephew Anemero Dekeri who is currently a mega businessman in Nigeria.

Uncle Sunday continued to talk about the one who has someone to look up to also has something to give. It was a special occasion for everyone to celebrate togetherness like the one who returned home after a long sojourn around the world.

"Baba's two-story building," Sunday pointed in the direction of at the upstairs, "was the first of its kind in the whole place. People from all over, far and near, came by to admire the house."

Talk of Baba—Uncle Sunday referred to him as Father—brought those memories of status, promise, and audacious times when Father instilled the spirit of winning like a "champ." The talk echoed with the ingrained theme to strive forward. Sunday summed it all up, saying, "Baba came from nowhere, but he made it. What about you, who has a road to follow?"

The house was the majestic structure of its time. New developments have outpaced the structure, which the older folk still remember as the embodiment of the grandiose and inspiring achievements of our father. Baba and his sons lived in the two-story building, and the women had their separate quarters. The two-story house had a corrugated zinc roof with two projecting pinnacles decorated with stained-glass windows of different colors. The building exterior was plastered with cement and painted, and the front of the house had rows of flowering shrubs and a green grass lawn.

Akhamie's Old house on the left annex by the modern house built by Agbierere's (Oldest brother) son, John Osikhemekhai Akhamie

It was the last house on the main road for those departing the village. The few other houses in the area were built with mud-red soil and thatched roofs. Baba's was the first house when coming to Afowa from Iyora.

The two-story house still carried the scars of burnt rafters from the wild bush fires. During one of the last destructive harmattan wild fires in 1966, a majority of thatched houses located within the quarters—Oguolomi—were burned to ashes. The fire also destroyed my mother's thatched building that she shared with the women, amongst others. It was in the heart of the dry season, and the fires carried by the harmattan winds from the adevo—the grasslands—wreaked havoc.

No life was lost in the fire, yet the property loss was huge since half the village's homes were destroyed. Families left homeless moved in with relatives while the massive rebuilding effort began. Under the shadow of the constant menace of the more bush fires, the village was forced to switch from thatched-roof houses to corrugated zinc roofing to reduce the damage from the fires.

Mama's Bungalow

My siblings and I were not quite old enough to build our mother a house. Baba, who was aging beyond the strength of his prime, had to build a separate bungalow for Mother. The symbolic action of taking care of family, as it is said, was the half-word "piece of advice given to a child." Baba said, "I may be old, but as long as my heart beats with life, I must complete my obligations."

We made red bricks from the red soil dug from a pit at the far side of the compound. Men using shovels, picks, and axes to dig up the red soil, which was mashed bare-footed. The men were paid for digging the topsoil to expose the laterite—red soil—and for molding the muddy mixture into bricks. Still, as little boys, Philip and I joined in the work. Mother and Peter, who was old enough, would fetch water from *Ederuae*—the kaolin pond—during the dry season when the rainwater dried up. Oghie and Lucy, my sister's housemaids, came to help.

Before concrete cement blocks were introduced to the village, all the houses were built from the red earth. It was a labor-intensive project to excavate the topsoil, which was comprised of sand and rubbish waste, to expose the red earth. Once the red soil was reached, it was dug and mixed with water before it was molded into blocks.

The manual work was nice when many people joined to help in mixing the mud, especially when the children were enticed and the work was organized as playful exercise. Although it could be fun for the children, it was difficult to get the team to stay on for long, and once in a while a parent would call their child to join in, which meant there was no one to play at the mud-work. The adults were serious at work and would have to complete the mud building in sections. Once the foundation was in place, there was an urgency to complete the exterior walls and install the zinc roofing prior to the next raining season. From foundation to roofing, the entire process was completed during the dry season because the red mud is susceptible to being dissolved by rainwater.

The mud-blocks stayed in the sun until they were dried into solid bricks, which the bricklayers used to build the walls. There were few moments of fun for us during that time of agonizing manual labor. I remember playing in the red mud, which was similar to porridge, with other children while making bricks.

Mother's house rose quickly from the foundation and was roofed with zinc roofing, but many of the rooms in the interior remained uncompleted and unused for a very long time. The building was completed with five rooms; Mother occupied two of the rooms and the remaining ones were vacant. The vacant rooms had no ceilings and were exposed from the bare mud and brick walls to the hollow roof.

The two rooms that mother occupied were finished with a special ceiling called *izeh*, which was constructed with hard wood supporting a mud slab with an open attic above. The space was used for the storage of food and stuff from the farm. A wooden ladder—*igbanaka*—was used to climb up to the attic. The use of the attic in such a manner made sense because it kept the goats from eating and tripping over the foodstuffs—gari, groundnut, rice, etc.

It was tasking to keep the goats from eating the food, because like dogs, they were part of the family. Mama had one special goat that lived with us for many years. Names were not given to domestic animals, and Mama's female goat did not have a name, but even so, everyone in the household knew which goat belonged to each person. After many years Mama's goat did not have any kids, because she was too old. But Mama would speak to the goat, especially if it forced its way in to eat the yams.

"Mama, you are talking to a goat," I would say. "Mama, it is just a goat, and it does not ever understand what you are saying."

Mama remained undeterred but continued talking year after year to the goat until it was sold at the Uzairue market.

Imagine, a mother speaking blessings to her goat! How much more for her children and family!

Cash Allowance

Money—i.e., coming in contact with money—was not an easy thing at all, especially for the young people. Doing some chores did not yield rewards because it was expected as a child's normal duty. Odd jobs were few and were hard to come by in the village. Several times I was tempted to steal money from Baba, but he was extremely careful not to leave cash around. When I was bold enough to ask for some, he would ask me, "What do you need the money for?"

In trying to come up with a response such as, "I want to buy sweets," I got stuck, unable to find suitable answers to his question.

Food was plentiful, but we craved sweet things which we could not grow on our own. In desperation, I devised a way to combine salt—which was plentiful—with sugar, which was not. The combination—two or three cubes of sugar and a sprinkle of salt—would be put in a bowl of gari Such a dish was an unrealistic solution.

Baba was well off but was no spoiler of children, and he was wise in the way of money. The only way to get money from Baba was to come up with well-reasoned plan. However, he would not stop anyone who applied oneself to make money. He would not seize the money from anyone who earned it. There is a saying, *"obo miele"*—meaning it is my hand that I eat—which is a way of saying that the one who worked by hand enjoys the fruits of his labor.

When I was about eight years old, I joined other boys to perform after-school farm work. The women were not expected to dig with a hoe and would pay the boys to do it. So it was an opportunity for the younger boys to earn cash.

This labor for hire—*"adogo dey,"* meaning the "buying evening"—was available for anyone who could use a hoe. Those in primary school years III, IV, V, and VI would perform such chores, usually during the months of January through March. The onset of the heavy raining season meant the ground was loosened up, so we were able to plough using hoes to dig the soil into columns of ridges for sowing crops such as beans, cassava, groundnuts, and vegetables.

Before adogo dey, my effort to earn cash was an entrepreneurial venture of firewood. The venture started when I was about six or seven, during my first year in primary school. I joined the boys to scout the nearby woods and forest for dead trees. The dead branches were cut into logs and tied in bundles. Early in the mornings, about 5:30 to 6:00, we would carry the bundles of firewood on our heads and walk towards Jattu. Once we entered the township of Jattu, we would walk slower and listen for customers' signals.

The buyer asked, "How much? How much for firewood?"

I started with a high price of two shillings, knowing I might end up with a fraction of my asking price.

"I give you fifty pence," the lady bargained.

"No. One fifty." My offer was troublesome. Too high! I wanted sell my firewood because other boys were selling theirs.

Philip, who carried the heavier bundles, bargained and also answered questions concerning whether the wood was good.

I was upset that they heavy load of wood on my head was not getting any respect. "How much do you want to pay for my wood?"

In response; the woman said, "I pay one shilling and *itolo*."

An itolo is the old three-penny coin denomination that was replaced by the five pence. Before long, selling firewood to make money became a busted joint venture for Philip and me. The business did not go quite as well as I hoped, but I learned valuable lessons. Apart from the hard work, the task of saving money and keeping records must be done. If we had given the money to our mother, it would not have been spent before Christmas, when we needed the money to buy clothes and shoes. But each of us selected a sponsor from among the women within our house to save for us.

"Here is my money," I said after the morning greeting every day after making a sale before returning to Mama. Each of us would walk over and hand over the cash. At the year's end, our savings were not enough to purchase the things I had wished for. I confided in Philip, "I regret not keeping Mother as my banker."

I learned firsthand the lesson of holding one's parents as the closet of friends before going to another person. Since then I have saved my earnings with Mother or joined the *adasi*—savings pool for family members—which was under Baba's control.

Agbirere; meaning "they do not beat/kill a visitor"—was the name given to our eldest brother. Following their settlement at Afowa, the family—Father and Grandfather—decided that they must acknowledge allegiance to Afowa.

Brother Agbirere (deceased)
The Family base/pillar
Agbirere Akhamie is the first son of Akhamie Osigwe. The name was given in order honor the village of Afowa – Uzairue, where the family resettled after departing Osigwe's home at Uloko – Uzairue. Agbirere was instrumental in view of his close working rapport with his father Akhamie. Agbierere's effort is noteworthy in establishing roots of the family at Afowa before his death at the prime of life. John Osikhemekhai Akhamie Agbirere's son attended higher institutions in Nigeria. As a businessman and industrialist, John has established many businesses at Akhamie's compound.

Agbirere was next to my father in the family ranking order, a capable man of valor, a sawyer, businessman, and the family pillar of support. He led as a quiet man but worked with Baba and the other brothers as they ventured into the forest, felling the mighty Iroko and mahogany trees. As the Iroko and mahogany trees were disappearing quickly from the land, Agbirere had begun to travel on trading trips and to places like Ogozima for seasonal farming. Agbirere provided the core leadership support for the family as the firstborn, strength for strength, was a no-nonsense, *"push me I push you, God no vex"* kind of man, and was gifted with creative wisdom and craftsmanship.

He ventured into the trading business and traveled to distant places like Onitsha in Igboland to buy goods. On the day the lorry arrived, the goods would be off loaded. The following day would be spent unwrapping plates, kettles, pots and pans, and a host of shining household items.

The things had the distinctive fresh smell of the foreign fragrances of boxes and wrappings. The front of the two-story building would be temporarily converted into a trading mart, like a giant yard sale. The village folks were attracted to it because of the new things and would come around to inspect everything, searching for bargains. However, everyone knew that the big sale was at the Uzairue market.

On the eve of market day, the goods were carefully packed and loaded into the cargo space of a chartered lorry for the big market. The majority of the work was done by Agbirere and his younger wife, called Anima, and some of their grown daughters.

Agbirere had two wives, as well as grown children who had families of their own, and children and grandchildren about my age. He lived but did not reach his full old age before he was killed in his prime in a motor accident while returning from Ibadan. The sadness at Afowa was heartrending. As one would expect, the emotions were mixed. There were suspicions that someone was responsible for his death. The customary ceremonial burial rites were an ordeal for our father, who had to bury his first child. Family members returned home from the city to console each other, even those who lived in far distant places.

My grown brothers took over the wooden bed I shared with Philip in our father's room, while we stayed in our mother's quarters. Following tradition and customs, Agbirere's property, including the two wives, belonged to Anabi. The traditional rites were performed and the two widows—Sametu-Onaele, the one from Elele, and Anima—were given in marriage to Anabi. With these two new wives, Anabi now lived with four wives. Such a tradition is called *ukku*, meaning for one to receive an inheritance not by will but by tradition.

Agbirere was the firstborn and leader of the Akhamie family. As the saying goes, "one must be sure of himself to challenge the Afe-Akhamie." (The family of Akhamie.) Everyone grew up knowing he was our leader, the one who paved the way. Without an outward show of strength, he showed us that strength comes from courage.

In the days of Agbirere, everyone in the village knew to watch out and "not to let Akhamie's sons observe willy-nilly, because they learn fast and create their own."

He was the leader who worked with Baba to acquire vast expanses of virgin jungle at Afowa. Fearlessly, he ventured into places in the jungle that many would not go to cut down tall trees for timber. Agbirere expanded his reach to the place called Ogozima—somewhere in the vicinity of the river Niger—in order to farm the virgin lands there.

We wandered about the genius and courage of minds and realized the answer was as much in our heritage as that of Grandma Okhee, who was determined her only child would not be taken from her. The same determination was passed on to us. Agbirere was the family's pride, like the prickle of marvels. Sadly, he died in the prime of life.

My father did not talk too much about the loss of his first child but mourned in silence for a long time. All the dialogue going back and forth was in his mind. The funeral was done as it would have been for a great elder in the village. The entire time Father watched in a silence of agony because he could not partake in the funeral of his son. It was a dreadful thing for the superstitious society who blamed the death on witchcraft. I had many questions regarding the death of Agbirere. "Was it the wives, Mother, or Father who was responsible?"

Chapter 6

Mama, "the Humble One from Okpella"

Imagine a young girl having to grow up in the same house with her future husband, along with his three wives and their children!

"I came to this house as a young girl. I was younger than you or maybe about your age." It was how Mama talked about her situation. She said, "I made do, so there is no use complaining to me as if I do not know anything." She always gave straight-to-the-point advice. "In spite of the circumstances, I always sought the good side."

Such a situation allowed her to tackle life's challenges with humility, and she was happy to tell the stories to inspire us, her children, since no one else knew, or cared, for that matter.

As a young girl she was sent away from her home to live at Osigwe's household at Uluoke. Her mother had given birth to four girls before their father passed away at a young age. Since her birth mother could not raise the four girls as a widow, she agreed to give Amina away to be raised as a child-bride.

In those days, without an organized foster-parenting system, children were raised by relatives in different villages. The people believed the child might become lazy when pampered by the parents. In some cases, however, young girls were legitimately married through arranged marriages.

During her visit to Uluoke, our grandmother Okhee was said to be really charmed by Amina, the young girl from Okpella. She described her as well-mannered. Mother repeated the story of how she came to Afowa. It was a way of instructing us on the realities of life. The story would conclude with Mother saying that when she became of age, she became the fourth and youngest wife of Akhamie.

The marriage of a girl-child was a customary practice. From Mother's account, her uncle must have made some prior arrangements with my father's family. Around the tender age of eight, Mama said that her first journey, after she left her mother, was when she was taken to Osigwe's relatives at Uluoke—the first village in the Uzairue clan when one travels from the Okpella clan. While at Uluoke, one day a fair-skinned, stout, and beautiful woman visited the house. The woman, she later found out, was Isametu, one of Akhamie's wives. When Isametu was departing, Amina overheard someone mention that a message was to be delivered to O*kpele*—the "slim one."

"Tell Okpele that she is a very good girl," Mama overheard.

About five days later, a dark, tall, slim lady called Okhee came to the house. When Okhee was leaving, Amina was asked to put on her clothes and accompany her.

"It was how I came to your father's house. I did not know where I was going. I did know what arrangement my uncle had made for me. At the time I could not disagree or agree with anything that I was told to do."

From that humble beginning, Mother said, "I took it as a personal duty to be respectful always of Uwewe. To live in harmony, fully engaged, and to care for the one who raised me.

"I stayed in this household from about the age of the daughters of my future husband until I matured into a woman. I have a world of respect for Uwewe as the mother who raised me."

When her children came into her life, Mama repeated the story of her life and commitment. "I will never make the same mistake that my own mother made. I will never abandon my children. I will raise my children." Routinely, she reminded us of that. "It is because of us that I stayed at Afowa."

By the time I was born, the problems between Mother and her family at Okpella had been resolved. The dispute was not because of the anguish of being given away. There was another conflict between Mother and her family at Okpella which almost ruined everything after the birth of my first two siblings, Paul and Cecilia. While still an impressionable, young, susceptible woman, Mother's resolve was tested during a dispute over her marriage.

The surviving uncle decided to claim his rights as the one to decide her fate. The uncle declared that Amina would have to return to Ogute-Okpella, where she was to be remarried to another man. According to tradition, the uncle could do these things because he was the only surviving and oldest male relative. The sticky matter then was whether she would be remarried to another man at Okpella, since he was entitled by birthright to his brother's children.

"My uncle claimed that I had to return to Okpella. I did not want to think of getting split from my children."

Under prevailing customs, Mother's uncle was correct in his assertions, no matter how flimsy it may have seemed, and whether or not it was for money. However, tradition also recognized the woman's right to make a self-declaration. A self-declaration resulted in the severance of parental rights and protection. When Amina was asked to decide for herself, she said that she would remain with her husband. Her children would not be separated; they would be able to grow up together as a family. A self-declaration cannot be overruled.

From the various ordeals as a young girl, our mother fashioned her own ways, fostering a positive persona and ensuring that her children did not become caricatures of negative nicknames. Mama became a

Christian and ensured all her children were given biblical names, such as Paul, Cecilia, Peter, Philip, and David.

David, my Christian name, coincides ironically with the native name that my father gave me, Ekhalevhe. It meant "greatness is not hidden." Also there were such praises as, Ogieneni, greatest king; *Ogie luku luku*, great king with a mind for greatness; *Odala u biele*, shinning blackness, and *Eluku*.

My a middle name, Aleghe, came from my mother's light-hearted nickname of "Mama Aleghe." But in the adjoining compound of Ayemoba's house, there was Patrick Agunu, who was also called Aleghe, which was a new trend for the last child born. He was called Aleghe, as was I, and I was confused by this because I heard my mother referred to as "Mama Aleghe."

The women exchanged glances as they let the matter fester for the moment at my expense. Later on I was told that Patrick found the episode to be quite amusing. "You Aleghe, me Aleghe, we are Aleghe together." I was used to one having many names, and I accepted the new realities of allowing women to have their way. "I am Aleghe, as the lastborn, and so I received my official middle name, Aleghe.

My mother would not spoil any of her children but took care of all the real needs of parenting. Unlike other boys who had sisters to help around the kitchen, I was given responsibilities I did not like. "Do not complain because you wash dishes. You do not have any sisters to do it. You must learn how to care for yourself. Nothing is wrong with a man who knows how to cook," Mama explained.

Mother did not have much but never shied away from giving whatever she had to others.

"Mama," I would ask, "Why do you always give everything away?"

In response she would repeat the same answer as before. "Because of you. I give for your sake so that one day, when you are in need, someone will give back to you."

I didn't understand what my mother meant at that time, but now

I understand her comments to mean "plant or sow the seeds in the hope that they will come back as fruit." Occasionally, she would take time to elaborate on our talks, "I was barely your age when I was separated from my own mother. I did not know much. Everything I know I learned from others. When people talked, I would hide out of sight, but I would listen. It was how I learned about life."

There was the bitterness of being abandoned and not being raised by her mother and growing up without any siblings. For many years Mama did not want to have anything to do with her mother at Okpella, but she was fond of her youngest sister, called Aneboku.

I came to know about Aneboku before we met because of my interest in my mother's family, which was greater than that of my siblings. I did not follow in the same trend as my siblings but decided to establish close contact with my mother's side of the family. I met my grandmother from Okpella when she came to visit and again when I visited Okpella before she passed away. Mama was also very close to Sunday Dekeri, the lastborn of her mother. Uncle Sunday became the bond which reunified my mother and her siblings as they become older.

Mother and daughter made peace and enjoyed each other's passion in the simple things of life. The oldest surviving sister lived for over 90 years before she passed in 2016. Uncle Sunday remained as the link to our relatives at Okpella. I treasured Mother's ways of retelling the stories of her life which revealed the real meaning of her humble virtues, love, and forgiveness.

My paternal grandmother, Okhee, was the parent who nurtured young Amina like her own daughter while Amina grew up alongside Okhee's own daughters. Anima was about the same age as Okhee's daughters, and she remained in that household from the young age of about ten until she married my father, when she dedicated her life to raising her children.

Mama Uncle Sunday and aunts

RIVALRIES OF THE WIVES

Mother was the youngest of four wives in a large household entrenched in spousal rivalries, but she chose the spirit of kindness. "A sheep does not fight with the goat, but when the goats fight each other, the moment there is food, they join to eat," she would say. Learning from the close companionship paved the way for me to seek her insights on many of the profound traits about her life.

"I did not have a childhood like other children who had someone to guard them," Mother said. "However, I grew up as a conscientious person. I listened to the words of wisdom from Uwewe. In this, your father's house, I was mistreated at times. One of the other wives attacked me and ruined my hair that I had plaited."

"Who was it that mistreated you, Mama?" I would ask.

"It is not child talk, for you can go around telling others. It is not good for children to talk bad about others. When bad things happen, maybe no one knows who did it, but God knows!"

It could have been any of the three senior wives, but I couldn't settle on one. The three wives equally were aggressive characters known to be quarrelsome for no particular reason. Yet they were our mothers.

"Everyone knew how troublesome things could get, but we were always conscious not to do wrong to anyone, because it will always come back to you. Make sure not to make any enemies. Choose to be the peacemaker!"

I persisted with a number of inquisitive questions, but she preferred to focus on inspirational stories. But many of the things were too much to ignore. I was disturbed by the notion that she did not eat the yams that came from our father's farm, and I was bent on making things right.

Notwithstanding that the yam was the staple food, I pitied Mother's situation of toiling strenuously while having to go without food. It was unfortunate that she endured such hard times in the house, especially since it was one of the more well-off homes in the village. She hardly complained about anything; however, it was distressing to hear her empty stomach growling and churning for food.

I asked, "What prevents you from eating the pounded yam? Why do you always have to cook a separate dish for yourself?"

Mama admitted, "I got very sick and was this close"—she rubbed her fingers and squeezed them tightly—"so they warned me that I would die and leave my children behind." Hearing that she could have died said it all for me, because I would not have been born without her.

"If I were to eat of the yams grown by your father, it would make me sick. I cannot be a sickly person. I have to be strong."

Mama believed she got sick because of a curse and jealous retaliation, but she would not mention who the person was who did such a thing. I was left to figure out who was the bad witch that was messing things up at our house. I settled on the idea that Mother was forbidden to eat the yams from our father's farm.

Several times I revisited the situation with Mother getting sick every time she ate pounded yams from our father's farm. I made a last effort to convince Mother to change just after she became a Christian. However, it was one of those matters that I decided to let alone. I respected the firm stance she took for her own well-being to ensure she was able to raise her children and see them to adulthood.

My attention was then diverted to her slightly bent fingers.

"No, I don't have any pains," she told me.

However, the one thing she used for instructing life lessons was the scar on her chin under the jawbone. "The swollen cyst on my gums from a toothache eventually went through the jawbone, so I have the scar. It was one of the severest pains I have ever endured."

Mama experienced episodes of toothaches. Without dental care, she believed it was the power of God which allowed her body's own immune system to heal those diseases which could have killed her.

"I survived many things to see my children grow up, so I give thanks and praise God every day." Mama believed she was alive because she was protected by the grace of God.

"When you have faith in God (*Oghena*) the Almighty, nothing can defeat you in life, not hunger, sickness, or jealousy of others." She recollected though, for a moment, and continued, "I asked God to heal me when I was sick. If it was water I drank, the water healed me. Water and herbs were my medicines." She rubbed the top of her chest. "I had a cyst in my breast. It leaked out and I was healed. Nowadays, my prayer is for God to protect my children. God will guard you through life. God will save my life for me to raise my children, which is what I live for."

Perceived from my simple outlook of life at the time, I said, "Mama, you have sad stories. How come there was no one to help you?"

Mama would turn those sorrows and pain into a positive outlook. "There were no hospitals. There were no medicines to cure many of the ailments. Do not to blame anyone. I want you to know these things so that they will inspire you to focus on the good and to stay positive. You must look at the good side of everyone. Do not concern yourself that other people dislike someone."

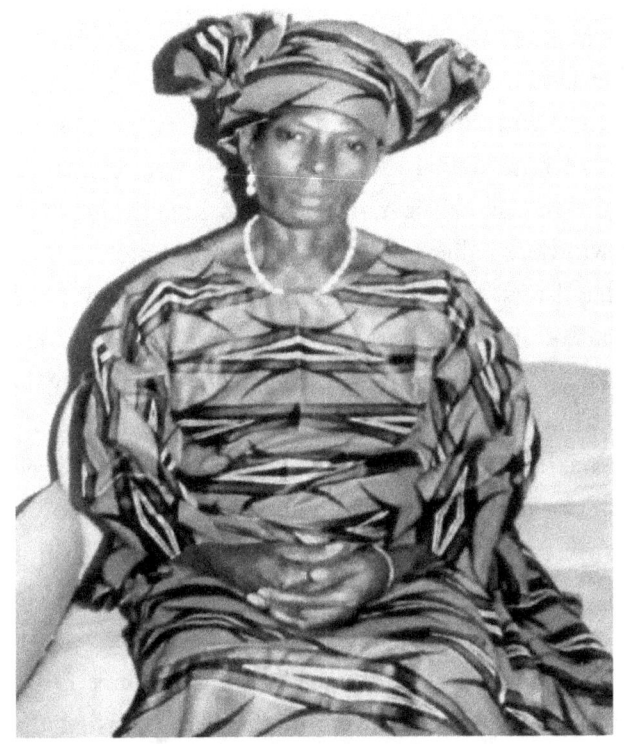

Mother Amina Celina Akhamie
Humble one from Okpella
Look straight at the face and her earring to see the distinct, colorful imprints centered from the corner of her lips to her mouth and between the upper and lower lips. Look straight at the face and her hear ring to see the distinct, colorful imprints centered from the corner of her lips to her mouth and between the upper and lower lips.

Mama was a physically beautiful woman. Not only was her beauty physical, but she also had the beauty of her personality. She had two very distinct marks of beauty—similar to tattoos—on her chin. They shone and sparkled in vivid, black-bluish colors, forming unique features on her face.

Unlike the Yoruba and Hausa, the Edo ethnic groups did not practice the art of facial tribal marks. For me it was one of those missed opportunities to talk about many other positive things that must have enhanced Mother's belief in the goodness of people.

My older sisters Anima and Ayemhekulu, and my brother's wives also had tattoo beauty marks, which were more obvious because of their yellow complexion. The markings were likely initiated by Grandma, who raised the women as her own daughters.

Mother's earthly possession was her love for her children and family, which remained steadfast throughout her life. The house was never locked, just in case someone should come when she was not home.

There was one drinking pot—made of clay—with a cup, situated at the enclosed corner of the hallway to the sleeping area. The leftover food was placed in the sleeping area of the bedrooms. Drinking water was scarce in the village, a situation that has persisted up until this day. The big pot of water was always covered, and the cup stayed on top of the cover. I was happy as long as there was water inside the big drinking pot from which we would get water for my father. Also, as the youngest ones, Philip and I were responsible for taking prepared food to Paul and Peter upstairs in their rooms, since they had become men.

Due to the difficulties of getting fresh drinking water, it was not to be wasted. The main pot and drinking cup were not washed after each use. You got your drink and placed the cup back on top of the pot. The next person used it and replaced it for the next. The fresh water was kept in the big pot made of clay, but after few days the cool environment encouraged mosquito eggs to hatch. The tiny larvae did not scare anyone, and it was not a problem to drink them. Everyone knew they were not dangerous until they matured into adult mosquitoes.

When the drinking pot was empty, it meant going on a trip to the stream to fetch water or going to my sister's house, where they had running tap water. Neither of these situations was an easy chore. If the choice involved going to my sister's house, it meant one would have to carry a bucket or pail of water on the head and walk through the entire village to return home. Going to Ugholomi, on other hand, was a major task involving a trip through the woods and jungle. We were sensible enough to avoid situations where we had to fetch water.

In the kitchen Mama had a grinding stone on which milling, grinding, blending, and mixing were done. The bigger stone, which was the main one, was mounted on solid clay about three feet off the kitchen floor, and on the top was a smaller, round stone for the grinding. The grinding stone was washed before and after each grinding and then covered with a flat wooden board. Each grinding stone might last over a decade, based on the amount of daily use for preparing meals. Through the grinding process, essential minerals such as calcium from the stone were added to the family's daily food.

Firewood was used for cooking. The firewood was collected from the farm and brought home and used in a fireplace with a tripod for holding cooking pots above the fire. The specially designed clay pots used for cooking were gradually replaced with black, steel pots. When it came to the chores around the kitchen, either Philip or I was assigned the chore of picking up and washing the dishes before dinner. There was always the inevitable bickering over who was supposed to do the dishes. Philip was able to sneak away from the kitchen and would time his return when dinner was ready.

I learned cooking. It was also during those moments of listening that I gained insights into some of Mama's profound traits. I would take over the yam pounding, a small gesture to relieve her from the strenuous pounding with mortar and pestle. The yam was boiled until it was soft then it was poured into the mortar while was still steaming hot. The pounding continued with repeated motions of raising the pestle high and hitting it on the yams inside the mortar. It was not just pounded; the yam mixture needed to become a smooth mixture without lumps. Being able to make exceptionally well-pounded yams is an art mastered with practice and patience. The pounding was one of those wonderful aspects of the village life which required one to engage in exercise before eating; thereby fostering an active, non-sedentary lifestyle.

The actual cooking involved knowing how to make different varieties of soup from many ingredients. Mother was awesome at cooking various dishes such as:

Egusi: (the famous) was one of my favorite dishes and was cooked often. It comes in several varieties such as with bitter leaves, *efor*—green vegetables—and mushrooms. The bitter leaves—egusi—took longer to prepare because the leaves had to be washed thoroughly in order to remove the bitter taste. Mama usually assigned me the chore of preparing the bitter leaves for the soup, so I scrubbed until the green water turned white to remove the bitterness. The groundnut/peanut soup and bitter leaves—which I was forced to prepare later in life—is an acquired taste.

Ogbono: (the-smooth), or drawing soup, is a frequently consumed dish which also comes in different varieties. It requires dedicated patience and skill to prepare.

The one common ingredient for the different soups is locust bean seeds—called *ugba*—and onions, salt, water, and oils. The family did not eat much pepper, so mother tried to balance the taste to the satisfaction of everyone. The smell of the locust bean, due to fermentation, is unpleasant. Many children tried to avoid it, but we could not avoid the seasoning after it was ground. Apart from the smell, another problem was that the fermentation of the locust beans makes it look like rotten cheese. Without toothpaste and daily brushing, despite cleaning with chewing sticks, one had to be careful not to be teased by other children as the one with ugba, locust beans-breath.

Eating fresh food from the farm or gardens and homemade meals ensured that everyone possessed thriving immune systems to ward off chronic infirmities. As such, the mothers were the naturalist and holistic experts in caring for everyone in the household. A noteworthy example involves the versatility of a plant-like palm tree that provided multiple uses: its kernels for red palm oil, the palm mantle—*ugburi,* candle—and many other types of cooking oils. Brooms also came from the palm tree's tiny branches. Mother used the mantle as substitute for kerosene lamps. Before the era of electricity, the palm-mantle was the popular lighting for the house and was made from the residue derived from refined palm oil. The surplus was sold to neighbors for cash or exchanged for other items.

In essence, Mama shared many of those things she learned from Uwewe Okhee, my paternal grandmother, including the use of the different herbs, spices, and minerals for nurturing a healthful lifestyle. It was the customary practice of the older folks to pay homage by honoring the water pond called Ederuae.

As children we only saw the pond as the murky, chalky water that was not potable unless it was purified with alum. Mama taught us about the usefulness of Ederuae for its healing purposes and for the varieties of minerals and soil types found in the area, from light-white sand to dark-black clay. The different soils were used for different purposes, including the sharp sand used in building. According to tradition, the oldest women were responsible for mining the white kaolin deposit and the edible clay found in the vicinity of Ederuae, the white kaolin river.

The people called the edible special soil *Elumhe,* which was well known to the children, who were given a tiny piece of Elumhe for treating stomach pains. Elumhe was also popular among pregnant women, who consumed it to alleviate the effects of morning sickness.

When the oldest woman died, it was passed on to the next woman in succession. The edible clay, which resembles dark chocolate, was mined by Mama when Uwewe was the oldest woman in the village. Also, the kaolin mined from Ederuae was used as wall-paint decoration in the native houses.

In periods of about six months, or yearly intervals, the native homes were repainted with the clay soil mixed with water into a paste, which was then smeared on the walls. I realized how commendable it was that Mother learned those various ways of life and traditions through the humble acceptance of her mother-in-law, which she also passed onto us.

In regards to the worth of Ederuae; one must separate the superstitious beliefs from that which has been confirmed through science. The myth most often recounted was that a yellow-skinned woman came as a guest. The fable claimed that the woman warned that ashes from the fireplace must not be thrown at her. The myth claimed that ashes were thrown on her, and she became angry and turned into the lake, which eventually flowed away to settle at Ederuae. The first time I heard the story, I dreamed about the mighty river that I had never seen which seemed to flow as it shrank in size. There must have been some semblance of truth to the movement of Ederuae, as I have observed the remains of mud houses along the outskirts of the Afowa-Iyora road. The area served as a cemetery at one time. The people must have moved farther away from Ederuae.

It was not mere superstition regarding the healing powers of Ederuae, since I have realized from scientific research that the soil in the area does contain dozens of special minerals. The Europeans came to explore the area years ago and encountered several of the mineral deposits. They posted a notice at the road junction to notify others of their findings. The signboard was there for many years until it succumbed to the elements. I could not read it then and do not know what the notice said before it was destroyed by the elements.

The Unforgotten Wisdom

Amid traditions where the man was the head of family, Mama was the one who taught me the duties of being a modern man. "You must know how to take care of yourself," she told me. She taught me how to cook and make sure others around me were fed. Although Baba hardly ever came to the kitchen—it was deemed unseemly for one of his status—Mama knew we were living in a world where everyone, man or woman, had to be independent. The men around me would give orders to get things done, but Mama was the one who engaged in conversation and listened. She did not feel insulted but calmly maintained, "Hard work will not kill you. It will make you stronger."

I listened quietly, allowing her to gather her thoughts, as it was considered good manners for the child to listen.

Mama continued, "If hard work killed, I would be dead by now. You see how hard I work and even do extra when I work for someone else."

I listened, waiting for an opportunity to ask questions.

"Do not look for trouble, but challenge yourself to do well. Take the time to clearly say exactly what you want to say. Always give to others, even when it is hard for you to give."

Mama continued to give advice. "I give now so that it will benefit you in the future, so you have to accept people and be able to share with people you don't like. You will go far and beyond, as far as your vision and dreams take you."

I had a coach in Mama to reinforce my oral history training as I learned the native names for time, days, week, months, and years. The Anglo calendar had already replaced the traditional calendar, but I felt that it was a nice thing for me to learn the native ways. First, Mama explained that the sun was used in the day to tell time. "At dawn, before sunrise, is six to eight a.m. When the sun is directly over the top of our heads, it is noon. And the sun goes down at six p.m.,"

Mama instructed me. At night it was the moon's *uki*—rise and fall—that counted as one month. Mama explained that the native word for "sun"—*ele*—was the same as *eleh*, meaning "today." The native word *afoaaki*—a week—meant the "time in space" between the market days of Uzairue. There are eight days in an afoaakiin the Uzairue clan, as opposed to the seven days in an Anglo week. I came to realize that Mama was teaching me many things that many people and children my age generally no longer cared about.

Mother must have learned many things about Western influence over traditional rituals through worshiping as a devoted Christian. She observed the Sunday worship but respected the traditional native's day of rest—called *Elewo*—and respected the Muslims' Friday of *Izumah* or *Zuma*. For many years Mama accepted all people and modeled her life on her past experiences as well as the influence Western culture was having on life near and far.

Chapter 7

The Changing Culture

The sixth year of primary school was the final year and the final push for teachers to prepare students for secondary school. They had to make sure their pupils could speak simple English. The students who learned stories through the native vernacular were encouraged to repeat the stories using English. We had periods of free time when classes A and B were joined together to allow students to mingle. That is where the teachers said our stories had to be told in English. I have a story in English, which was told to me by word of mouth and which came all the way from Ghana:

> Once upon a time, there were five dogs. They were raised by a family to do menial jobs around the house and go hunting with their father. After many years, the bounty of the land had been reduced to scarcity, and there was not enough to feed families during the long famine. Some may have died of starvation. The father took all the dogs for hunting in the forest and did not find any meat to bring home for the family. They traveled far and wide and came to a river to cross to an unknown land.

The hunter said to his dogs, "Well, my boys, I am old and there is famine in the land. It is time for me to release you, for once you cross over to the other side, you may have freedom."

There was a little grumbling and whining, and in response, the hunter continued, "We all know what we have here, but over yonder is the unknown. I promise you, life will be better in the unknown land far beyond the river." One of the dogs said, "I want to stay with you!" The hunter said, "I am not driving you away."

All the dogs had excuses as to why they did not want the cross over. The oldest said, "I can't get my nose wet." Others decided it was a trick, while others were outright disobedient.

Among the five, the smallest one decided to venture into the river. Once he jumped in, a raging storm swallowed him up, and he disappeared. Kwaukua was the name of the little one who was gone forever.

The hunter and the other dogs returned to the famine-ravaged lands, where later the hunter died.

A song that went along with story says:

> *Bele Bele; come here*
>
> *Bele, Kuku; come here*
>
> *Ala, Bato, come here,*
>
> *But the Kwaukua kwua sit down.*

During the time of plenty, Kwaukua was singled out for the most severe tasks and often mistreated. When it was time to eat or do pleasurable things, Kwaukua was not allowed to join in. The years of loneliness and mistreatment taught him many survival skills. Bele, Kuku, Ala, and

Bato were the big dogs who were treated as the favorites in the family.

When it came to crossing over the river, Kwaukua, who was used to hardships all his life, had no ambiguity in his choice, since he knew that anywhere else would be better than the life he had endured. Kwaukua, malnourished, was grounded on the shore of a land of plenty, and he prospered in life and later gave birth to the new generations of dogs we have today.

The stories of entertainment were venues for teaching about life. The short story about the five dogs and the song were easy to commit to memory. The story was about us, human beings, and our God-given talents. Much is expected of everyone, but many fall short along the way and refuse to "cross over" to a better life. In later years I have become aware that our universal understanding is the creative talent for developing our evolving human ingenuity.

The Change of School Year

It was a period of rampant changes in the Nigerian educational system. I recall the many years since the Biafra War and the loss of the Catholic schools when the government took ownership of them. In the midst of the changes, the old Demonstration Primary and St. Peters schools were combined into one school, and students from both schools had to attend the same school. The old Demonstration Primary School was no longer used for teachers training and it was now called Afashio Primary School by default, since the two schools had become one. The people of Afowa felt disrespected to have the neighboring village's name posted on the school. Such insults in a society where "the name" is crucial sign of identity could have deteriorated into confrontation between the neighboring villages. Afowa had to petition the Board of Education in order to have its name put back on the primary school.

Something that was supposed to be as easy as changing the school's name became an unwelcomed nightmare when it took months of negotiating back and forth with the authorities. In the end of the drawn-out struggle, the village won because of help from the educated, younger generation. It was decided that the power of knowledge must be recognized. The elders did not read and write, but they showed the way through their wisdom to organize and strategize with their children, who had the knowledge through education to accomplish their goal of maintaining respect within the Uzairue clan.

Although I was spared the transfer to Demonstration Primary School in the last year of primary six, the entire school year was changed to six months—from January to June—in 1973 instead of January to December. For the first time I was united with all the students in my village in primary six.

Towards the end of the school year in primary five, the prospective high school candidates were expected to enroll for the Common Entrance Examination (CEE) to be admitted into secondary schools. Without guidance, many students missed the opportunity to move forward.

Some of the students who were clever in my class did not take the CEE as required for admission into the high school, and some repeated primary five instead of moving to complete the sixth year. I sat for the CEE but was registered for the lower-rated high schools: St. Peter Grammar School at Agenebode, and the secondary school at Okpella. I received letters of invitation from these schools to report for interviews.

My older siblings wanted me to attend Our Lady of Fatima or St. John Secondary School, but they did not talk about the matter with me. It was a period full of tension as I tried to retain likes and dislikes.

I learned to accept the situation I found myself in by relying on those words Mother espoused, using her life as example. "You can be humble and face the realities. I am not able to get you what you want, but learning to do for yourself, along with any help you get, will make you go farther," she told me.

Once I became a student at Our Lady of Fatima, I was issued complete sets of uniforms, notebooks, and school supplies, but I remained disappointed that I did not have sandals to make a complete uniform. Without the sandals, I managed to avoid walking barefoot on the asphalt-paved road by wearing any shoes I could find. More disappointing was not getting to stay at the boarding house. I could not stay there, since my parents had stopped taking care of my schooling expenses.

Those were difficult times when I thought my family was unaware of my needs. I also had to recognize it was one of the most important lessons I could learn. As I joined the other day students to walk three miles each way, I was forced to hold onto the vision Mother espoused, that "No matter the circumstances, one must always focus on the good!"

David Akhamie

PART II

IYE KHEE

Iye khee means "I say," which is a common phrase unifying the dialects of the Afemai people

Chapter 8

The Enduring Codes

Neighboring clans within the Afemai cannot understand each other's dialects. Words can even have different meanings from household to household within the same village. The culture allowed for creative ways in which everyone contributed to the expansion of the language. However, we were seen as one culture. There was, however, one commonality: i.e., people speaking *Iye-khee*.

The nurturing indoctrination of the young ones in our ways ensured the survival of our traditions and heritage. Perhaps due to our experiences during the era of slavery, disobedience was frowned upon. It was thought that the child who did not listen would grow up as a worthless person (iyeye). Body language was a highly regarded method of communicating coded words, as shown in the greeting of "Good Morning."

Oral folktales recount the era of abduction when people were captured and sold into slavery. In songs it says, "The whites captured folks and took them to the house of suffering;" and in response, coded words were introduced. When someone was aware of the kidnappers, they used the coded words to disguise real messages. One prominent code that has stood the test of time is "Nah-bgia," or "run in the morning".

Nah-gbia. Everyone knew it meant "run into hiding, the abductors are lurking." Those who understood knew exactly how to react: the way to avoid being captured was to run.

At the farm, when it rained, we ran to the thatched hut located in the mid-section of our farm. We took cover there from the rains that would last for hours. If the rain lasted for a short time, we were able to shelter under a big tree or among the plantain trees. During the raining season, we spent lots of time in the hut and we would listen to the older family members during such moments of leisure. If the parents did not want to talk, they allowed the oldest person in the group to talk. Everyone knew the saying, "Children are seen but not heard." This was a reminder that a child should be smart and learn our ways by listening to their elders. When the rain lasted for hours; we roasted corn and pear (olomi) in the fireplace.

One such time, my oldest brother, Agbirere, broke the silence and told us the following story.

There was a man who had five sons. This was a very long time ago when they caught people. ("Catching" people is a reference to slavery.) Strangers appeared at the farm. The visitors were those who wanted to take the famer and his family away. These strangers could not speak our language. They had personal guards as escorts who understood the Iye-khee of Afemai, but they were not adept in the local dialects. The accent of the guards was the giveaway that they were not native speakers.

> The visitors were expected to bring back only one or two people, but the family was larger than they could handle. As it was raining kind of intermittently, the farmer told the family, "We have to find food for the visitors." The

father told two of the boys to go for yams, while he told another to go for corn.

He said, "Go out and dig up the yams. You, harvest corn. You, get more firewood so we can prepare some food for the visitors to eat." Meanwhile, the father was pointing them to a designated route of escape, signaling them to return to the village.

The smart sons read the parent's eyes and knew when it was their turn to run away and escape. The two boys sent to go and fetch firewood understood the signals. But the farmer had one wayward son who kept his eyes on the strangers, sneering, and missed the signals. The father nudged him, saying, "Okpo, go and check on your brothers!" But the son didn't stop; instead, he stayed, still watching the visitors.

The father stepped out of the thatched hut and called out, telling boys to hurry. To his wife—he called her Onaigbah, meaning "the one who runs in the morning!"—he said, "Go and help the boys bring the firewood. It is wet and we do not want the visitors to catch a cold."

"Yes," she said and walked away.

The man said, "I am coming to help with the yams. Hurry, you, keep digging for yams." As the farmer walked away, he kept trying to signal the family to run away.

The kidnappers heard him and yelled, "What is taking you so long?"

The boys were already halfway home to alert the villagers. One by one, the family avoided being captured. All except the headstrong boy who disobeyed and missed the signals that would have saved him. He was taken, never to be seen again.

Within the Afemai, reciting fables—called *abguzo*—was a way of spending leisure time and entertaining young ones: The fables and songs contained codes for those who were able to decode these secrets.

The Afemai have been endowed with plenty, so they believe it is "only the fool who goes hungry."

Abguzo—meaning. I have a puzzle.

Ahney!—meaning I am ready to interpret a puzzle.

If an older woman calls, "abguzo," the response is "ahney."

You've messed up if you do not answer, "Ahney."

"What if a man married a bad woman?"

"He would keep her to have children and find another good woman who would listen and stay by his side."

"Yes, finding a good wife is the duty of the mother of a man."

The Uzairue have a saying that it is a terrible woman who looks for trouble. The same analogy applies in the saying about a wife who cooks and does not share with her husband.

"Yes, she must put her hand in her butt to pass gas (*Naey efu ahsha*)."

"Even the worst person is desirable to someone.

Abguzo. "Does anyone know why chickens do not have teeth?"

"The chicken does not have teeth because, like children, they are stubborn."

The chicken, as you know, was very stubborn, always lazy.

One day a message came that God wanted to see her.

"Tell God that I am busy now. Also, God should first tell you why He wants to see me."

God sent for the goats, the fishes, the sheep, the cats, and the dogs, but He told them not to show their teeth to the chicken until everyone had received theirs.

"What happened?" everyone wanted to know.

Oh, yes! The chicken noticed that everyone was eating, smiling, and grinding.

She was very upset and went straight to God. "How come everyone has teeth, but I do not? Do you think I will bite the others?"

God said, "I called you first, but you refused to come."

In the spirit of acceptance, no person is helpless and no one is left behind. Stories and songs are the vessels with which new generations connect with their ancestors, thereby making certain that the memories of our ancestors remain within the family from one generation to the next.

Chapter 9

The Village Pride

Since the era of the Biafra War, things have continued to change as the villages got larger and the population grew. Most young people my age attended elementary schools. Those of us privileged to have a secondary education were considered to be the ones who benefited the most. We experienced farming with our families during childhood years but changed to the path of exploring education as the springboard to future endeavors.

Social Gatherings

Villages took great pride in their young people when they returned from school during the holidays. Social gatherings were planned for those who attended high school or college. The students who returned from other towns would have learned something new to bring back to the village. During the holidays, schedules were carefully planned for the parties in order to prevent any conflicts between the villages. Afowa and Afashio often shared the same location—the primary school building or the missionary church premises—for their parties. Planning mainly consisted of collecting money from students in the village to buy refreshments.

At the parties the students would recite poems, riddles, songs, and jokes. Others engaged in mathematical calculations—like solving calculus equations—to win prizes. The social events were not open to anyone attending elementary school, but we managed to attend the parties anyway since word of the elaborate planning always leaked out.

I was one of the youngsters who climbed up to the windows in the building where a party was being held in order to see the boys and girls dancing. When "Dance, dance, dance" was announced, all the boys would get up and walk over to the girls to request a dance. The girls were invited to the parties, so they did not have to contribute towards the cost. The parties were opportunities for students to perform whatever acts they had prepared to make them popular. Some would sing lyrics like, "Music, I say, is a universal language; music, I say, is a universal language. Of all creation, there is nothing like music."

The music was played on a record changer that was borrowed for the occasion. This was the era right before disco music and the music played was mostly American and Jamaican artists, mainly Jimmy Cliff. Everyone loved music and sang along when songs like "*Ofege*"—by a Nigerian artist—were played.

CELEBRATING CULTURE AND TRADITIONS

I shared in the wonderful experiences of my culture when the majority of traditional ways were still intact. This was in the '60s before the Biafra War. Traditional dances were performed during ceremonies. Each of the villages had their own style of dance, although the names of the dances were the same. At Afowa and in the Uzairue villages, the *isoko* dance celebrated the hunter. I did not have to go far from my compound to fully experience the isoko, since my cousin Oshiomha Idalu was the greatest hunter of the time.

Once, seven days after killing a buffalo, a celebration was held by adult males, and the isoko was the main dance.

I was awakened by the hustle and bustle. I ran over to where the noise was coming from. The women were pounding yams. What a sight in the early morning. Two women stood facing the steaming, giant-sized mortar, taking turns pounding on the boiled yams in the mortar. Each woman raised her pestle at alternate intervals; one pestle went down and landed on the yams while the other was raised.

I looked for my mother, whom I could not find among those pounding the yams. I said to Imaatu—Baba's wife number three—"*naigbia*. Good morning, Mama!"

"*Nah na!*" she replied, but she was not really paying attention to me because she was absorbed in scooping the boiling hot yams from the oversized, black steel cook pots. A fire was burning under the giant tripods that held the pots; everyone looked quite busy, as if they were cooking for a battalion of soldiers. It wasn't the time for an impetuous child to be lurking around. Fortunately, I saw my mother with the crew cooking the egusi soup.

By 9:00 a.m. the cooking was done, and there was plenty available to feed the entire village and guests.

Our compound, which extended into Oshiomha's, gradually filled as people, old and young, assembled. There was a special drum called an *ube,* which had been hollowed out of soft wood and covered with sheepskin. A group of three to four men beat on the ube drums. Each man held his drum under his legs in a squatting posture and beat on the drum with his hands. Another group played a hollow steel drum. As the drumbeats rose to higher levels, the leaders of the Ogbalege clan, dressed in full hunters' outfits, came marching with their guns. They were few, but they were accompanied by an entourage carrying the tail of the buffalo, bows and arrows, clubs made from long sticks, and antique guns. As they paraded toward the arena, they sang the salutation song, "*Ilomi somi agiode. Olo lo agiode.*"

As they sang, each of the Ogbalege displayed his unique gyrating maneuvers. They walked around in a circle and stamped in unison, which made the ground shake. After the Ogbalege had done seven rounds, Oshiomha was dressed as a hunter.

The hunters' real costumes smelled like the musty jungle, with blood and sweat stains that made them look like different men. They carried Oshiomha shoulder high and paraded him around with an escort of hunters. They sang in a rhapsody like rapping, their dance steps and faster cadence narrating their encounters in the wilderness.

Esi—Celebrating Ancestral Propinquity

Afowa celebrated esi festivals each year which rivaled the modern celebrations of Easter, Christmas, and the New Year. The word *esi* refers to the guardian angel/spirit of our ancestors. An esi festival, such as the new yam festival, was in honor of our ancestral propinquity. Like Thanksgiving in the United States, each village honored God as the ultimate creator of life, and thus, we dedicated special thanksgiving celebrations in His honor.

The village elders would purchase a big cow, which would be tied to the kola nut trees at the utukue, the village square in the area in front of the chief's compound. The ground would be covered with green leaves that had already been cut from nearby coconut trees. Information usually spread person to person as to the day the cow would be killed. From my house to the village square, I would join the other kids and adults to gather around the cow at a safe distance.

The men walked out a well-planned strategy. The first man would come from behind and grab the cow by its tail to distract it. Two other men took control of the horns. There would be a little struggle, but within a few minutes the animal would be forced down to the ground on its knees.

Some of us would shout, "The cow is going down."

"Hey, move the head," the people would shout, and the exposed throat would be cut with a sharpened knife. The blood was drained into a giant-sized bowl called an *italabi*. The blood would be cooked and then consumed. The group of men skinned the cow and cut the meat into portions. Not a single piece of the cow was thrown away. The skin of the cow was used as hide, and all the meat was cut into small pieces and shared among the families to cook and eat.

The days of celebration continued in a buzzing atmosphere until afternoon, when every living soul who was able would come to the utukue to watch the festivities. The traditional dances of *iyabana, ilo,* and *idogu*—designed to reign for all eternity—were performed. The *igelegede* dance of Afowa was the equivalent of acrobatic break-dancers of today. The igelegede included frequent gyrating moves for the young girl dancers with flexible muscles. The performance did not last long after the girls were married. It was discarded before I went to elementary school and it was never revived. It was truly an exciting dance, comparable to American cheerleaders' routines. (Google Edo, Etsako, Esan, Okpella, etc., and the word "masquerades.")

When the esi festival or one of the major ceremonies was near, the elders held private discussions, which were then broadcast by the *okabor*—the town crier. About 5:30 a.m., the okabor would walk from one part of the village to the next, telling everyone the schedule was set.

The town crier would shout, *"Ika rena ma so, yeh khe Erameh kha ma so-ooo.* In the coming two market weeks, the elders have set the date for the celebration of esi, *akogho* (night vigil on the eve), and so on and so forth.

Okabor—Town Crier

The planners of such social events usually paid very little to the village crier, as no fees were required to broadcast the information. The village crier served the culturally vital role of broadcasting news, information, and special events. Whenever a person had information to pass on to the entire village, the person would have to inform the crier, who would verify the accuracy of the information and obtain the chief's approval before making the announcement. Usually, the family celebrating a marriage, or announcing a burial, or wanting to thank the entire village for something would inform the crier, who would include the piece of information in his morning or evening rounds.

Akowe —Learned One

The village elders had their individual roles, which were based on their unique talents. The village scholars, known as Akowe, were responsible for transactions in English and keeping the village records. They helped in writing and reading letters, which was the main means of communicating with people in faraway places.

My turn as a writer came because as I was a stay-at-home student. My customers were usually the women in my house. They would receive a letter from a child in the city and would come upstairs to my room so that I could read the letter to them.

When one of the women came to my room, I would know that it was time for me to do some 30 minutes of letter writing. The woman would pull a seat close to where I was studying and produce the letter, perhaps recently received from her daughter. I would read and translate the handwritten letter into the Afemai dialect. "Your daughter says, 'Greetings,' and she hopes everyone of family is doing fine at home. The children are doing well. The baby started walking."

We would have a conversation about the letter, or she would start asking about things that were not in the letter. In the majority of letters, there was nothing new and nothing much to translate. Then the woman would have me write a letter for her, mostly prayers for everyone and her prayers for long life and prosperity for the person who had written the letter. After reading the letter and writing the reply, she would bless me and express her gratitude that she did not have to leave the house to find another person to read and write letters.

Even though I performed this service for the women of my house and people in the village, they did not start to call me Akowe or

Iticha, which means the "learned one," like my senior brothers. People viewed teachers with respect, but I saw teachers living a life of desperate hardship.

Not knowing where life would lead me was a big concern and caused many anxious times. I lost some my smile and cared for very little. I hated the idea that my family had not produced someone who had graduated from a university. My fathers' house, with its grandeur of the past, was falling. The village was losing its luster as our parents and elders were left high and dry so that they looked about themselves with stony, dry faces.

Life was changing to selfishness—an "everyone for yourself" philosophy. The only thing to look up to was earning a high school education, which was watered down and weak for lack of innovation in the educational system.

Obo—Native Doctor, Priest of Oracles

Some of the village elders were native doctors. They specialized in herbal medicine for healing, and some served as priests who interacted with the unseen world of oracles. Becoming a good native doctor and a master took a long time and gradual learning from the elders. The various crafts were represented in the village, but almost everyone had a farm and other skills to make money.

It dawned on me when the elders were passing on (to join our ancestors). The sons and daughters had disregarded their parents' wishes to carry on with the traditions, and they had rejected the ways of old in preference for modern-age life. Modern education must accept its share of blame in the rejection of our traditional ways by teaching the tunnel vision of Western culture. The first traditions to go were our native music and the act of storytelling. No one danced the isoko for the hunters, since the wild forest, home to the animals, was becoming scare. *Izi agba-azi*—the dance of Izi—a woman's dance was replaced with high-life music, and blues, disco, and reggae serenaded the villagers in the night with strange tunes of "natural mystics flowing through the air," like the lyrics of Bob Marley. In the era of Christainity, the native healer of Afowa referred to as Ikhumetse; meaning the medicine heals has become less desirable for its connation of curing powers.

THE OCCULTS AND MASQUERADES

The elders were left, scratching their heads, wondering what was to become of our traditional way of life. Our parents' songs and dances, like the *Igiagbgede Oka khagbe*, had been forgotten completely, since there were no recordings of such events.

The last of the old guard and performers during my time were the likes of *Akhigbe*, Akowe, *Elegha*, and *Erhagbe* (the one-man masquerade/mascot called *Odogu*). They were top drummers who played the talking drums of *Ilo*. The performers, who had reached the age of our village elders, had children the same age as me. Their children went to pursue Western education like me and did not engage with their parents to carry on the traditions.

There were many occasions for the dance of Ilo and the main attraction of the Ilo, the masquerade of Odogu. The crew of four to five drummers would depart from their homes separately and meet up to make their way to the village square. Each of the drummers played a tone during the walk to the meeting place. The smaller drum set the tone and pace as the drummers played for the spectators—mostly women—who danced freely.

The drumbeat would continue then the biggest drum would join with a steady beat, announcing the coming of the Odogu— who would be dressed in full regalia—as they marched to the village square. Along the way, a string of cowry shells and bells tied to Odogu's ankle rattled and created distinct harmony, left/right, as he approached. Folks cleared the way and brave children joined in the fast-paced walk. The talking drum synchronized with the songs of *odede meh* as Odogu arrived and danced with the crowd of women. One of his favorite moves was to turn around to reveal his rear-end (ass) at the women, who danced fiercely and too close.

The performance continued as Odogu took over as the main performer. Odogu would cajole the spectators with many moves as the biggest drums intensified the calls for summersaults. After about an hour, Odogu would find his way to the extreme corner of the square as the spectators scattered to make way for him.

The signal would be announced by the smallest of the talking drums in a high pitch, and like the crash of thunder, Odogu would answer the call for multiple summersaults, which were usually triple flips. The thunderous reverberation of the giant talking drums has remained an unforgettable memory for me.

Ighaghazi

Afowa had a special masquerade called *Ighaghazi*, so-called because of the sound of big, hollow instruments. I was petrified the first—and only—time I experienced one of their performances when I was about three or four years old. I remember the dance moves, but the scariest thing was the majestic costumes. The unmistakable figures of menacing creatures were larger than life, tall and huge, and worn on the heads of the dancers. The masqueraders' costumes were feminine in appearance but were designed to conceal the real-life masculine identity of the dancers. The dancers had breasts but were masculine in strength, which they demonstrated by picking up any person standing too close in the arena. One had a little baby figure in his hand that was holding on to the "mother" dancer, but the dancers left no mistake they were real men dressed to resemble women. And their dance maneuvers gave it away that they were really men. The moves of dance were designed to signify life passing from the older to the younger generations.

The entourage was masculine wonders was called Ighaghazi; *Ibiba* represented the female and main dancer, followed by *outogo*, and another "lady," or the second "female" dancer. They were the strongest men in the village, selected based on their proven display of strength and physical prowess, but none of us knew their real identities, which was ostensibly kept as a mystery by the village elders. As spectators, we were blown away by with the spectacular display of womanhood and strength.

In 1973 a white girl came to Uzairue. I do not know which country she came from, or her name, but I guess she was most likely an American graduate research fellow. Anyway, the white girl was friends with Andrew Akowe, who was nicknamed "Raw Materiah." She came quite often to visit Andrew, who helped her to negotiate the purchase of the old masquerade costumes. Nothing was special about the sale, but it was hidden from the curious, eavesdropping ears of the villagers. I heard about the sale of the artifacts, which left me wondering what she did with a piece of our culture.

Osumah, Oshiomha—the Ogbaleghe, title holder—Abu, Odio—the *Ojo*—Obo, and other men who often gathered around my older brother Anabi started talking, and one of them explained, "The white girl, a stranger who was brought along to the village by Akowe's son, we sold Ighaghazi costumes to her."

"Osumah, do you know whether she was going to make white people wear those costumes?" one of the men asked.

"Well, it does not matter now. None of us was going to were the costumes!" Osumah said. From where I was eavesdropping, I picked up the clue that Osumah was one of the Ighaghazi of those days.

Anabi joked, "I cannot believe that you sold those costumes. You told me no one was wearing them because of the peppers, which the rats concealed inside."

"To be honest with you,"—I think Osumah was beginning to feel guilty—"I don't think the white woman was going to wear them. We were just glad to get rid of them."

Gone are the days when the chiefs—the title holders called *daudu*—and elders' blood would run and they would sweat at the sight of *Idogu* and *Agene*.

Depicts mother and child masquerade
The entourage was masculine voluptuous wonders
called Ighaghazi; Ibiba represented the female;
main dancer; followed by Otugo, and another
lady or the second female

For many years, what the white girl was going to do with those costumes remained a mystery, but I treasured my heritage and took pride in the people of the Uzairue clan. I counted myself as fortunate to have experienced one of Afowa's last, memorable yet majestic, vivid, and colorful Ighagazis. Its memory is vivid enough to be retained for life. To watch something so terrifying that one holds on tightly to the memory as an adult is indeed marvelous. It is unforgettable.

Ebenya's family were the flag bearers of the Ighaghazi. They were the distant relatives who shared the same quarters of Oguolomi. During the time, Oguolomi's quarters served as a last holdout and center of the village's traditional occasions, far more than the other quarters—called *edie* at Afowa—of Okotogua, Iyesimi, and Iyorfa (Afitakpe). As one of the last of my father's generation, Ebenya, as a shaman, reigned for a very long time as the native doctor and priest of the Inene shrine. After his death, his sons, who were supposed to carry on wearing the mantle, simply retired from such things. The younger boys of my age left home and went to the city to find a better life, saying there was no future in old ways.

ANCESTORS CALLED ETU

My age group and generation were the ones straddled between the traditional ways and the intervening Westerners' new way of life. The influence of the new era separated us from our beliefs that we were incarnated through Etu, our ancestral guardian spirit. With the coming of the Christians, we were given baptism and the Ten Commandments, and we were told that God is the only God, the alpha and omega who created all things.

Baba, who was not a Christian, prayed to Etu to intercede for us; through Osigwe, his father, so that our ancestors would grant good fortune and blessings on Baba's household. Baba believed Etu answered his prayers, since many new grandchildren were born in the household during that time. As such, my father believed he must give thanks to Etu at the shrine after the birth of each new baby. Once the mother regained her strength, she would prepare a delicious pounded-yam dish for the thanks-giving ceremony

Etu was not used to place curses on others, and our entire household dared not belittle its divine blessings. Like the ritual for new babies, there was a ritual every year to celebrate and give thanks for the yam harvest.

Road Construction

The Afowa area was very rural prior to 1974, when a main road was made with a bulldozer. The main road was shaded by huge trees planted on both sides of the road. Afowa was the first village in the Afemai area to engage in a major transnational business, transporting food commodities between the southern and northern regions of Nigeria. The road created an opportunity for Afowa to be connected to the country's main highways and for tractor-trailers to come to the village. The trade name for the company founded at Afowa was *Allah Dey*, a slogan that was posted on the Mercedes Benz transport haulers. They traveled from the Uzairue market, the main commercial center in the south, to the major cities in northern Nigeria.

At the time, the old generation of lorries—America-made Bedford trucks referred to as *Abeginodo*—were getting phased out because, unlike the Mercedes trucks, they were not suited for the kind of long distance travel needed in Nigeria. The old road to Afowa was not suitable for heavy haulers, and a paved road had to be constructed for the heavy cargo-haulers to be able to enter and exit Afowa. The village elders and business people commissioned a road construction project, which was given to the local businessman by the name of Arunah, a native of Ivbie-Okpekpe clan.

It was the first time I had ever seen the bulldozer called a caterpillar. The big trees were felled as the single bulldozer moved massive amounts of earth for the new road. It was a disappointment that the dreams of a paved road did not materialize as envisioned, but the road nonetheless addressed the need for commercial vehicles to come to the village. The construction also opened the road from Jattu, going through Afowa, Iyora, and Apana to villages in Ivbie.

After the road construction, the rapid pace of change turned Afowa into a different world from the humble life the village had previously known, just like my father's generation's attempts to preserve our old ways. The old ways became only memories in the minds of old teachers.

Modern Music

Music played a vital role for everyone, young and old. Children learned to sing, dance, and clap to music. Whether in times of joy or sorrow, music makes life sweet. My generation was the first to be influenced by Western music. As a youngster, I did not think this influence was a problem. It was the time of the prototype highlife music, which was a mixture of Western-influenced music.

The rise of prominent musicians, including the late General Bolivia Osigbemhe, originated novel folk music using the newly introduced Western musical instrument, the electric guitar. The music was recorded in sound tracks on LPs—i.e., "long play" albums—to preserve them and replay them whenever we wanted. Unlike the traditional performances which died out when they were no longer remembered, modern recorded music would last for long time to come.

There has been a resurgence of Afemai music with the new generation of musicians. Constance Young Bolivia, Young Jerry Oshiorenua, and others such as Benji Igbadumhe and Waziri were popular throughout the '80s and beyond.

A song is as good as the story it tells. Bolivia sings a song about a child's life being like a piece of cloth in the market:

Imami yea imimi, i mimi Kpha naba

I found the cloth that I like so much, my hand won't reach it; so, I will inform my folks and ask them to buy the cloth for me.

My mother who loves me will console and give me comfort…

The good thing about folk music is that even those who do not speak the tongue can hum along with the lyrics and dance to the music. The clans may have different dialects, but music unifies everyone. The dialects were not written down and were flexible for enough for anyone to include words in Pidgin. The songs were supposed to be passed on by word of mouth, but they have become a forgotten piece of our history.

Chapter 10

Adolescence and Growing Pains

As boys the chance to join in the hunting was exciting since one who went with the hunters was seen as brave. Anyone younger than 10 or 11 was not allowed in the hunting gang.

One day the plan was leaked that the older boys were heading out to hunt for animals that burrowed in holes, like rats and 'possums, rabbits, and snakes. Philip and I, along with some other boys, were able to join the group, and we hurried off along the footpath at the back of our house. On the way, the older boys noticed we were tagging along. They said we could not join them.

"Without a cutlass, machete or hoe, how do you expect to go hunting?" one of them asked.

"This is going to be a problem. They must return home before we go farther inside the bush," another one said.

They mumbled together, trying to come up with a ploy to scare us away. "The bad ghosts are all over in the woods; and they may chase us. You can't move fast in the bush, and the ghosts will catch you," they said.

Another one of the boys was more forceful. "They should go back home!" he demanded.

"Boys, return home," the oldest boy told us. "I will make sure we share the meat with you if we kill anything."

Philip, the others, and I were determined and were unmoved by such scare tactics. So they tried to outrun us to prove that we couldn't keep up with them. Their scheme was to leave us behind, and once they were out of sight, some of them hid in the bush. As we approached, those ahead pretended to panic, screaming in an attempt to scare us into returning home.

Reluctantly, we finally gave in. "We are not wanted here," Philip said sadly, and we turned around and returned home.

The hunting trips rarely yielded any game, but the camaraderie united the hunters as they worked together. My age group did not organize such activities before I left the village, but for others, those acts of bravery began in earnest from early age, with such daily activities involving the mysteries of nature.

The real hunting was by done older men. While we slept they scouted the forest and returned in the mornings with their kill. "How come they are not scared of the demons out there?" I asked myself.

"It has to do with what it takes to be a man. One has to be bold enough to venture out in the woods alone," I was told.

The hunters did not give up the meat from their kills for sacrifices.

The Mystics of Ugholomi

The closest river, called Ugholomi, was one of the natural mysteries because the water flowed from underground. Many of us had not seen big rivers before. It was a scary place, if not dangerous, because of bad things associated with water. It was a dreadful place that I didn't want to go to on my own.

It was an act of bravery to venture into the forests around Ugholomi alone, which I rarely did, usually waiting until someone would accompany me. Those days as a youngster were when indelible myths were imposed on my subconscious, which would be manifested in dreams later during my adult life. Such fallacies depict my youthfulness, as the place continues to invoke the mystical beliefs of those people who still regard it as place to worship.

Baba said, "Idavid, Iphilipu, go and fetch drinking water."

When it was my turn to fetch drinking water, I was willing to go in the company of others, although I was still hesitant. But it was not always possible to go with others, especially during the raining season when the stream would be deserted because there was an abundance of rainwater to use.

"Philip," I said, "There are no people. That place is awful. We can't go alone. No one will be there to assist in placing the pails on our heads." It was an excuse to conceal my fears.

"We have to fetch the water. There is no way out!" Philip responded, but his face showed his definite dislike for the errand.

The voodoo doctors had declared the area as the location for *izobos* (sacrifices) and the sacrificed items were displayed from bushes near the river for everyone to see. Placing an izobo on the pathway created the first impression of fear. A sacrifice was neither consumed nor taken away during the night, and it would stay in place until it decayed, often emitting strong, disgusting smells.

"How come the people worship idols on the footpaths leading away from the village?" I questioned. "What is so mystical about the areas along the footpaths that the voodoo priests prefer these sites to display their devotion?"

Silence begets silence!

The brave grown-ups went to the stream alone during the darkness of night to make the sacrifices. Izobos were grotesque, especially when the sacrifice was stained with fresh animal blood. Few talked about such things, which was how ignorance remained. No one cared to explain the beliefs of worshipping a deity by sacrificing dead animals. We just knew to stay clear.

"Mama, does everyone know that offering a dead animal as a

sacrifice will not resolve their problem?" I would ask, wondering out loud. But there was no answer.

The unanswered question was whether or not the offering of sacrifices gave the person making them any reprieve from their tribulations. *Was the person making the offering seeking long life or prosperity?* I wondered.

No one knows! No one was brave enough to tell the others not to believe in anything.

Human nature is susceptible to idolatry, just like those few who aggrandize ignorance by making such sacrifices.

There were no guarantees that making a sacrifice would give the person long life or prosperity. There has never been a concrete way to measure the benefits in a society where many do not live long, only long enough to pass on such ignorance to their children.

On the way to get the drinking water, in an extremely low voice, I said, "Sheesh! Look at that izobo! That is gross!"

"Ahaa, the smell is awful! Cover your nose," Phillip said.

With little pails balanced on our heads, we walked down to the river with reluctance, lacking the courage to disobey our father, and we endured being pestered by flies feasting on the izobo. It was not the time to show weakness or fear, but the unknown remained as a problem, just the same.

These were times when I wondered about the life my parents lived and how my life would change as I grew older. The people depended on the farms for sustenance and lived closely with nature and their surroundings. But despite the snakes and wild animals which could cause harm at any moment, we learned survival skills.

Dreadful dangers came not just from the wilderness, however. There were hidden objects that could cause injuries from walking on bare feet. Sharp pebbles—which pierce through skin—stinging spear grass, and species of earth worms that burrow in between toes to lay eggs were ever present. When we walked barefoot, the *iziga*—zigga parasites—infested out toes and the spaces in between, causing excruciating itching.

Schooling was every child's dream. It was a means of escape from the life of farming. For most, schooling was a welcome dream for both children and parents, but in the midst of the superstitious forces all around us, some stuck to the old ways. Others foresaw education as a means of indoctrinating the minds of children to give them a better future.

According to tradition, the fish from Ugholomi were not to be eaten. It was strictly forbidden to kill the fish. Years later, around the period when I was in elementary school, the little fish—mostly catfish—had grown larger. Still, no one dared to kill them. A story was circulated amongst the students concerning one oyibo—white man—who was warned not to eat the fish.

"That white guy caught the spotted fish, which he cooked and ate for dinner."

"Do you mean that the oyibo ate the fish from Ugholomi? For real? What happened!" I asked.

"He died shortly after he ate the fish," the rumors said.

"No wonder on one has killed the fish," I said.

"Yes! It has always been that way. No one dares to commit acts that would result in death."

I certainly didn't want to die, so I didn't press further. I never thought of killing any of the small fish after that story.

During the raining season, while the stream was less frequented by people, was the best time for the crafty and ignorant worshipers who used the pathways to hold their rituals for their idols. Whether the stuff was for sacrifice or a selfless act to revitalize Ugholomi, it simply conjured unpleasant memories, and it could be argued that it was a failed exercise for ameliorating any problem. The sacrifices varied from dead cats to goats, sheep, and household items. Sometimes, a tent was set up and the sacrifice placed inside.

Obviously, it must not be desirable, I thought.

After about two weeks, the dead animals disintegrated as nature took its course. Maybe the sacrifice was meant for nature in the first place. After biodegradation took its course of action, only the solemn imprint of the place which had caused so much fear was left in a child's memory. But through the natural decomposition of the dead animals, I realized that I didn't have any reason to be afraid of the sacrifices. And I learned in the Bible that God does not accept dead animals as a means of worshipping him.

Many of the voodoo priests have passed on and no one has replaced them. Their children do not follow the same traditions. Also, the forces of Christianity have begun to have a strong influence on our culture. Although the influence of the Anglicans had weakened, the Roman Catholics remained as the main Christian religion in Nigeria and their missionaries were putting down firm roots in our villages.

Those who still want to consult with oracles and voodoo priests have to travel farther away to other villages. The number of izobos have begun to decrease along the village paths and at the stream. Christians like my mother have had a complete change of heart, and no longer believe they should offer sacrifices to deities for their children's sakes. Mother told us children that, as a Christian, she would not consult oracles nor perform izobos. Rather, Mama committed our lives to God in her prayers. She prayed, "Protect my husband, my children, Agbokhiavho, Emosi, Agbaso, Philip, and David. Do not let evil things come near to them. God, You are the Creator of heaven and earth, and all things belong to You. We are Your children and all life is on here on Earth to serve You. Our Father Almighty, let me live long enough to raise my children."

Mother's strong faith as a Christian influenced us, her children, to embrace Christianity. Like Mother, who was the first to join the church, Peter followed in the same fashion and joined the Catholic Church. As a mass servant, from then onward he remained involved in church activities.

"Amina; how long is this going to continue? Every morning you are out of house," Baba said to Mama.

"We went to church to serve God," Mama told him.

"I am not against serving God. But for you to be out every morning, you and Sametu-Onaele, is not acceptable."

"We sent the children to school and to be enlightened in the modern ways. The least I can do is support them in the new ways."

They talked over the matter of going to Jattu for church in the early mornings.

"There is no turning back," Mama promised. "I have rejected the worship of idols. No more! I refuse to consult oracles and perform izobos."

"How come they have live chickens grazing all over the area, but no one is killing them?" I asked

"Those were the chickens used as sacrifice. The cock was the only chicken acceptable. The cock was for conveying masculinity. Many of the chickens left in the forest after the sacrifice survived and grew into beautiful cocks."

Young chickens have replaced the really grotesque stuff, and in a way that is progress. I have seen hens with little chicks roaming the wild. Someone must have failed in their sacrificial attempts to pacify their idols, thus introducing the hen to the forest. It is amazing that the villagers—perhaps out of reverence for the idols—have not caught the wild chickens. Maybe it is matter of ownership, or maybe it is actually tough to catch them. I would think the stubborn kids would have gone there to round up some of the chickens. But superstitions are still there, and no one from the village would want to find out what would happen by stealing any of those chickens.

So the chicken population has grown and it serenades the days in the peaceful jungles. But such practice of bringing chickens to Ugholomi was not a practice while I was growing up in the village.

I did not ask, but I knew that Father was a pragmatic man, because once we passed through the fetish sites of sacrifices along the footpaths, we did not see them anywhere close to the farm. It was as if Father were saying, "Working hard and taking care of your crops is how to have surplus harvest."

Our farm reflected the changing traditions with the abundance of fruit such as mangos, *ogi* —which taste like apples—avocados, oranges, soursop, and other varieties of tropical fruit. Anyone can eat as much as the mouth can chew and the stomach can contain. But fruit does not last in the stomach like yams, and we did not see it as real food. By midday Baba would have harvested the yams, which he boiled with the skin on. The boiled yams were for lunch.

The mystical life never seemed to cease as we returned home with heavy loads on our heads. One day, along the way, we saw the Fada—the Reverend Father, the priest—who was walking alone. The priest was dressed in a white cassock, covering him from his neck to his feet. As he strode along, his brown sandals pushed forward in a right/left rhythm that exposed his legs. With both hands he held a book and read as he walked by.

"Good evening, Fada," we shouted as he walked past us. After he was out of hearing distance, I asked, "What do you think the Fada is doing, reading along the road?"

I was told in no uncertain terms, "Fada is chasing away the evil spirits."

I thought I understood the reason he didn't respond to the greetings.

The Night Entertainment

Evenings under the bright, shining moon provided time for leisure. The men rarely spent the evening with the family after dinner. They usually gathered at the front of the house, while the women stayed with the young ones inside. On rare special occasions, Baba stayed around to tell stories about the interesting places he had travelled, such as Lagos. On those nights everyone would gather around the veranda, listening in awe to Baba's stories.

"Go and bring the chair for me," Baba said in soft voice, just loud enough for the two of us to hear. The chair was a special folding chair called utequi-ukpo, which resembled a hammock. It was made of special cloth and served as a comfortable resting place before bedtime.

Under the hospitable brightness of the moon, everyone was welcomed to the veranda. Baba rested on the hammock chair, within hearing range of the conversations. One by one the women brought out their four-legged stools called igiokos. There were chairs, but the women each had their own special stool to sit on. Each woman would bring out a bowl of sun-dried melon seeds to be shelled. The girls would join in—occasionally, with reluctance, the shy boys would too—in order to share in the stories and laughter. I showed my skills in the undeclared competition of removing the dry skin from the melon seeds.

The moonlight brightened and seemed bigger during the cool, dry season. Then the boys would head out to the neighborhood playgrounds. The sand, piled about five feet deep, served as a natural cushion for landing on during wrestling matches. Once I was old enough to leave the house, I would sneak out to enjoy the hoopla, but when I did, I missed out on many of the stories being told at my compound.

The mischievous wrestling often caused fights to erupt among the boys when somebody got angered when the play grew too rough. There were downsides of the nights' playgrounds, such as when the boys would pee on the sand to make a mud-like concoction, which would then be carefully lifted and thrown at unsuspecting playmates. Such incidents were tightly held secrets that nobody reported to the adults because the one who did would be banned from future games. On those nights at the playgrounds, we also looked out for any chance to play with the girls.

I said, "Philip, last night you missed hearing many stories."

But Philip always found a way turn it around. He said, "You missed out, because after you left the dance of idu-pedu opegbu, the girls came out and danced so close. Every boy had a girl as a dance partner."

"Oh, no, I did miss that." I said, feeling I really had missed out. I was left wondering how come things always happened during my absence and why Philip was able to have such wonderful times as he described to me.

Philip and I grew up quickly and eventually grew apart in the things we did, especially when I started secondary school. I shied away from the sand games but was still able to chase the girls my age, who were beginning to show the full busts of maturity. Occasionally, I got wrapped up in the thrills of the fun and games—which were disguised a make-believe struggling—of groping the girls.

The girls would say, "Leave us alone." But they must not have really meant it, for the fun and games would always happen again another night.

Chapter 11

The Ventures of My Fathers

There was a shared responsibility of fatherhood among the older men. The majority of the elders like my father must have lived over 90 years. That is just a rough estimation. In our household the fathering duties were shared among the older sons of each of the four wives. Paul as the oldest of my mother's children, was seen as Eramha—the father—but Baba still gave the orders.

Fathering responsibilities were taught at a young age. Baba taught patience, since it was not easy accepting the traditional ways of having the oldest male in each family as a father. Baba spoke few words but used idiomatic expressions to remind everyone of this tradition. One such reminder was naming one of his granddaughters Airumedafe, which means "one does not compete for head of family."

Baba used his life as a way to coach each child to make his or her own decisions. He believed that doing the right thing and working hard would bring one a place of leadership.

I complained to him, "Baba, I have not received the better treatment of my older siblings. I have to buy my own clothes."

Father's way of speaking was profound without adulterated words, and his words carried the full meaning to the listener. He said, "The one who is in the jungle does not remove straws from his head." It was his way of saying, "I know the times are changing. The influences of the white world are very real. Take my advice, which will stand the test of time."

As I listened to such reflections, I realized he always maintained an unruffled demeanor. He had high regard for our ancestors and always called on them for support.

"Osigwe!" Baba would call out to his departed father when he stumbled, unlike Mama, who called, "*Nilah kasi,*" meaning "blessing."

Baba followed the old traditions and would bless his father, Osigwe, and his departed ancestors. "Osinegba," Baba would call to the almighty, "Take care of my children and do not let any harm befall them."

As adolescents, the boys gathered around father's quarters to eat dinner from the same bowl. We sat on the floor and surrounded the bowl of pounded yams and another bowl of soup. Father would wash his hands in the water bowl and pass it on to us as he prayed, "Osinegba, bless our ancestors," and he would call each of the departed by name. "Guide and protect the family."

He would cut a piece of the pounded yam, dip it in the soup, and place it on the shrine. Most of the time the piece of yam was small. He might simply toss it away when we ate outside on the open veranda.

Baba became the head of his large family and the breadwinner at a young age. Apart from farming, at one time or another during his life, he was engaged in basket weaving, shoemaking, tailoring, and traveling as a trader. He was trusted as the one to hold the money for the villagers, like a treasurer or a banker. He had a sizeable cocoa farm, which provided a profitable cash crop.

Yam was our staple food. The yams came in different varieties and could be eaten roasted in an open fire, boiled, or pounded. As was the typical custom for one of his status, dinner must be pounded yam and a soup of meat and vegetables. Yams were abundant and some of them were sold.

Traditionally, the farmer who produced the best yams was regarded as affluent, but the introduction of cocoa as a cash crop displaced the traditional regard for the yam. Among the popular varieties of yams were *obinna, abiede, enekha anehkedesi,* and *emhi-cho*—which were bright white in color—and the yellow yam. The best yams were the long tubas sold at the Uzairue market. It took special skill to stack the tubas in layers in two columns, which were then tied with a special rope. Like the varieties of yams, the ropes were named according to their purpose.

The one special water yam—called anehkedesi—had a yummy taste and melted in one's mouth. It was also the most suitable to be served during the new yam festival. The people have a saying when referring to the taste of the anehkedesi. They say, "The goat is waiting for nothing!"

When the yams were skinned, the peels would be left for the goats. The goats would notice the yams were being peeled and would gather around to eat the skins. However, the skin of the anehkedesi peels off, leaving no edible parts, so the goats would end up with nothing to eat.

Much of father's daily work at the farm involved tending the yam fields and cocoa plants. Yams were grown by every family to be used as their staple food, while the cocoa and other cash crops were planted in the fields as trees, which only the well-off farmers could manage. Unlike the yams, which were planted from the tubas, cocoa seedlings were purchased through the local agriculture representative, who worked for the local government. During the season of heavy rain, we had to take the seedlings to the farm for planting.

Our lives were sustained by farming. The planting season came after the hot dry season when the plants would shed their leaves and stay dominant like dead trees waiting for the next rainy season.

The social life and activities were fashioned according to the seasonal patterns of yam farming. The major traditional festival celebration of Esi is performed during the yam-harvest period. Most of the villagers did not plant cocoa, since it was mainly sold for cash and was highly labor intensive, all the way from planting to harvest.

Our father followed the tradition of the new yam festival and Esi, while the Catholic Church celebrated Easter and the harvest bonanza.

Easter Celebrations

Preparation at the church increased in the two weeks prior to Easter. The schools prepared students and teachers to march in the procession. With the exception of our fathers, everyone was fully engaged. In the villages of Afashio, Afowa, and Jattu, the old men who were church elders made a mobile tent which shaded the Fada from the sun. The school band got in on the action and led the way around the church, and one or two of the elders guided the priest towards the first stop at the village of Afashio.

Cecilia, my sister, said, "There was a story about an Afashio man who wanted to disrupt the possession at Afashio, so the Fada —the Reverend Father, who was a white man—said, 'Does Afashio always want the Fada to come there first?"

"No, the man wanted to disturb the sacrament mirror," they said.

"I am interested to know what happened to the man," I said to my sister.

She went on to explain, "The man went crazy. He said something from the sacrament mirror slapped his face. He was crazy and never recovered his senses."

I witnessed when the possession arrived at Afowa and was welcomed with a gun salute like it was an Esi festival. The crowd said prayers as mass was given at the village square, which was right in the shadows of the ancient shrine. The elders showed great respect for Christianity, even though it was responsible for the weakening of ancestral worship. Times were changing; it was an opportunity for us to learn about the Christian's world.

Rainy Season

For my father, the dry season presented its headaches, since many of the trees might not return to life, and some of them might have their roots eaten by voracious termites. One of the wonders that defy reason is that those termites grow into delicious delicacies. After Easter, when the rainfall has softened the earth, the edible termites, called *Ido*—stones—came out for their maiden flight.

"Debiedi (David), wake up."

"Naigbia (Good morning), Mama."

"Nah Na! Oh, my goodness, the stones are flying all over the place." Mama continued swinging the broom. "I am late getting to the farm. You go and kill the Ido."

"The sky is full of Ido," another parent warned. "Be careful out there, the snakes are out and are eating the termites."

I picked up a broom and a container half-filled with water and went into the fields behind the house to swat at the swarms of flying Ido. Once they were forced into the water, they were trapped; they could not fly away or shed their wings to crawl away.

Cocoa Farming

The harvest season normally falls towards the tail end of the rainy season, which implies that the more rainfall each season, the more the cocoa can soak up the water. The harvesting began when the green/burgundy/purple pods ripened and turned yellowish. It was fun at first but become real laborious because of the heavy lifting necessary to carry the loads from the farm to the village.

Meanwhile, there was excitement in sucking on the juice from the succulent cocoa. We knew to stop sucking the fluffy, fresh cocoa seeds when our teeth became sensitive and the juice began to taste sour. The manual labor of harvesting the pods without causing damage to the trees was left to the men. The pods had to be collected from each of the trees and placed in piles. From there they would be picked up and taken to a central location. One could break open each pod using a machete, but with thousands in the piles, we relied on the older family members to smash them more quickly using tree limbs.

Removing the beans was reserved for the children. It might seem like a fun job, but it was not. In order to get the seeds, the cocoa pod was broken to expose fluffy, juicy, white fruit. The seeds are collected in big baskets which allow the juice to drain out to be prepared for fermentation. The juice is collected underneath the baskets in bowls and is later shared among members of the household. Like the succulent seeds, the cocoa juice has a special, natural sweetness.

The inner parts of cocoa beans would be dried in the sun, unmolested by the goats and children because of the bitter taste. However, the dried cocoa seeds are the main ingredient in chocolate.

No one seemed to care beyond the sweet juice collected during the fermenting process that was shared for its refreshing taste. By the time the juice was gone, the fun of cocoa was long gone, and it was just hard work to dry the beans in the sun and prepare them for the market.

People in the village measured things based on usefulness. Banana leaves were seen as more useful than cocoa leaves, which were seen as worthless. A song in the Afemai dialect reiterated the point that "banana leaves surpassed cocoa leaves." In their judgment, many would rather grow bananas or plantains, which were for daily consumption. Needless to say, many did not see the connection between the cocoa seeds and the delicious chocolate produced by Bonita, Milo, or Ovaltine, just to mention a few of the popular companies that were established to exploit the cocoa beans for commercial uses.

Like many, my thinking was limited at the time, and I could not see the big picture of cocoa, which was that the money from the sale of it paid for my older siblings' schooling. I later realized the extent of the ventures my father was involved in by recognizing the chocolate as a final product of our cocoa beans. It was a mega international business, and people made large sums of money.

"Who plucked that cocoa and threw it in the tree over there?" Father would ask. Usually, no one would admit they had done such a thing. When I plucked the cocoa to suck out the juice, I made sure I got rid of the evidence, which usually meant burying the damn thing. The fear of getting caught restrained me doing such things often.

Baba, who knew how many pods were hanging on each tree, got upset if anyone plucked the ripe pods just to suck up the sweet juicy fruit and discard the seeds. He did not scold anyone but allowed us to learn how to be responsible. He often used his eyes, as if his eyes could talk for him, and we got the message.

The dried cocoa beans were bagged and taken to the market. Sometimes, a buyer came to the house, equipped with a scale to buy our beans at the prevailing price. When the sale was done at the house, we were happy because it saved us from having to carry the load of heavy bags to the market.

For many years, decades even, the business of cocoa was a well-organized Agri-business under the local governing cocoa board, which coordinated the farmers and traders. In the mid-west and western parts of Nigeria, the focus on agricultural produce diminished when petroleum money became the order of the day, and petroleum became the main source of revenue and commerce of the country. The result was that people abandoned their farms in droves. It became evident that sending children to school to learn the Agri-business so they could take over the family farm was a thing of the past, and it was better for the farms to die away.

Chapter 12

Our Lady of Fatima Boys College

The sheer beauty of the flowering evergreen trees was mesmerizing. They were full of life, some tall and flowering, others not, but all were lined along elongated, curved corridors. There were also many species of hibiscus and the magnificent Pride of Barbados planted in rows. The walkways had been extended outward to the green fields, away from chains of classroom buildings which followed each other in a seamless parade. The basketball court was situated almost in the middle of the campus and served as the assembly grounds. Awe at the sight quickly transgressed into daydreaming.

Oblivious to the fact that the whole class was focusing on me, I was transfixed in a daydream. A call from the teacher jolted me to reality. I was in class three then, but it was easy, after one look at the scenery beyond the windows, for anyone's mind to wander away during one of the midday lectures.

The imposing scenery at Our Lady of Fatima Boys College (later renamed Otaru Boys Grammar School) took my breath away the first time I ventured onto the campus for the admissions interview. In the same manner in which I was enrolled in the elementary school through Jokar some years back, a few weeks before the school opened

Our Lady of Fatima Boy College Auchi; picture taken in December 2017

I arrived at the school in the early morning, prepared for the unknown, wondering whether we were going to take a written test or have an oral interview. Pius appeared more businesslike than usual, and he left me at a spot along with two other boys. "Wait here for me, do not go anywhere," I was told.

Anthony (Tony) Akhamie, my nephew who had come from Igarra and was also seeking admission, joined me with a sigh of relief. We waited around and occasionally enjoyed the beautiful scenery.

"I am sure you don't know what we are supposed to do," I said to Tony.

"Nothing really. My brother told me to show up for the interview. I did not take the common entrance examination."

"Are you sure that you are going to be admitted?"

"I do not know much," Tony said.

We talked back and forth while Pius walked inside to the office. Through the efforts of Pius, we were among the first students to be admitted that year, since many were unprepared they were unable to catch up, with the switching of the school year from January to September. The news of my admission to Our Lady of Fatima Boys College was a source of pride. I returned home with expectations and began making preparations.

In view of the chaos in the country's education system, expectations were high for those of us who were admitted to secondary school straight out of elementary school. Many students were sidetracked into teacher training and other programs after elementary school.

Tony did not stay at home but with his brother John Akhamie in Igarra. As the only one in the village admitted from my class, I was the talk of the village. After I overcame the seeming prestige of my high school candidacy, the realities of academics in terms of learning began to dawn on me. I entered high school to experience a different world and exposure to the powerful acumen about society, socialization, cultures, geography, history, literature, religious studies (of the Holy Bible), mathematics, and the sciences, all taught in the English language.

"UNCIVILIZED"

The purpose of our schooling was to eliminate ignorance and make us civilized; however, we fell into the pitfalls of underrating others. The lack of inclusion of Afemai in the curriculum had an immediate impact on the weakening of native traditions. The students did not know the fables and songs of the Afemai. There is a saying: "We do not laugh at the one who was caught in the rain but make a fire to keep him warm."

The idea of seeing others as of a lesser social class was all around us, and it was reinforced by education. Such behavior, that one way was superior to another, resulted not in strengthening the culture of the people; rather, it eroded traditional ways, including the dialects—the native "tongues"—nutritional foods and herbs, native medicines, clothing; the list goes on and on.

The years after the Biafra War, and during the following years when I was in high school, were marked by the evolving way of life. While the teaching at school focused on the academics, the changes in the culture and traditions quickly taking place meant ours was a fading way of life. The trend was towards yearning for the enlightenment of the Western culture.

I was expanding my frame of thinking into the unknown, further away from the everyday life to imagining new places, people, and dimensions. However, I did not have a full understanding of my native culture. Walking back and forth from the village to Auchi, my mind and body were strengthened, physically as well as intellectually.

I often thought of the hardship of having to walk three miles every day from my village to the school. As I walked, I would reflect on the people from Ivbie. I grew up watching villagers from Ivbie-Okpekpe, who came to Jattu to the Uzairue market every seventh day. The majority of them—who traveled dozens of miles—were mothers and daughters carrying loads of clay pots on their heads.

It seemed their source of income was the handmade clay pots which were carried on their heads for the two-day journey on foot. The women traveled from Ivbie, a neighboring clan, to Uzairue through Apana, Iyora, Afowa, and Jattu. I had not travelled beyond the village of Iyora, but I could imagine the long and strenuous journey the Ivbie people undertook to sell their wares at the market. At times we regarded them as less civilized because of the mere fact that we lived in close proximity to the towns, while they lived in areas deprived of the influences of Western culture.

When going from the village to the farm, we usually encountered the women carrying the clay pots. The younger girls were naked, with the exception of their waist beads. Older women were partly dressed but were still exposed from the shoulders up. They spoke an Afemai dialect we could not understand.

From a distance on the winding paths, one could hear the women's voices; they were quite vocal. They had an expression—"*ukphae!*"—which sounded like a foul word (amounting to "fuck"). It was seen as uncivilized behavior for the Ivbies' loose lips to say "ukphae!" Such words would be met with rebuke from the older women. "*Noor pkha leh,* where you came out of?"

I recall that before the school age of five years old, children of my age group often walked around naked. I did not have any clothes before I started elementary school. But I was not the least concerned about being naked while I played in front of our house and was oblivious of the Ivbie women returning from the market. It could have been that the Ivbie women were admiring our house. But it dawned on me that my "thing" was the focus of the women's attention.

As for the Ivbie women, sometimes we passed each other on the way from the farm, or some may have recalled that I was the boy who lived in the big house at Afowa. With the passing of years following the road construction, things have transformed. The Ivbies' weekly odyssey to the market has been replaced with the use of lorries—the big Bedford trucks—that could carry passengers and goods. The old-style lorries did not have a key starter, and were started by a crank at the front bumper.

Through mutual regard for our way of life, I did not pointedly stare at the naked girls, which would have been seen as vulgar behavior for a boy. Our exchanges were limited to eye contact. However, I have distinct memories of the women who carried their clay pots, with both hands providing support. The girls exposed their breasts and danced in unison. The dark and shining black beauties with their heavy loads were something to behold. The hot sun would dry their sweat and often they would ask for a drink of water; sometimes, we shared such moments of good gestures.

At times the group would offload their clay pots, which would be carefully arranged by the roadside, and they would walk down to the stream to bathe and take time for refreshments. The journey to the market would take almost two days on foot, and the return journey would take more. Although some of the women might use the lorry transporters, still, it was a hard life for them.

For the most part, the journey on foot was made during the hours of darkness, so an opportunity to lessen the amount of strain on the body by riding in a lorry was a desirable option. I perceive it was likewise a thrilling experience for the women to see some of the nice buildings and electricity as they travelled through the missionary compounds.

Pottery survived as a tradition of the Ivbie-Imiahkebu people, but the clays pots became unprofitable when more durable metal pots and plastic materials became available as housewares and cooking utensils. As I walked to and from the eminently esteemed place of learning at high school, I was bemused by the fact that the economics of the Uzairue market and local entities were not integrated in the educational system.

The Lorry Accident

One day at about the age of ten, I decided to go to the farm alone after school. On that bright, sunny day, I walked from the house and went through the Ayemoba, Odamugo, and Agunu compounds, headed towards Adevo. On the opposite side of Aguna's house was Ikumetse's compound, where Kadiri Ikumetse, a colonial soldier and veteran of the Second World War, resided. It was the last house in the village. Someone mentioned that there was a crash at Atekha and asked whether I was aware of it. I shrugged and continued on my way.

I walked passed Adevo and down the slope towards Atekhai, which was the mining area. Atekha was always a scary place, since many have died there during mining accidents. Also, it was one of those mystical places for Izobos. The sloping hills and valleys contained mineral deposits, including the white sand and black and dark clay exploited for commercial purposes. Every few decades, the village lost young men each time the mine collapsed, and the blame would be placed on some unseen forces.

My senses were heightened as I looked for the accident, since there was no mining at the time. I continued downslope towards the valley. I did not notice anything different, but suddenly I was overcome with fear from the unusual sight of a middle-aged woman lying on the ground under the shade of a big tree opposite the path to the mine entrance. It crossed my mind to turn around and return home, but I was too close. As I reached the spot directly opposite the woman, I heard her moaning and saw the strain in her eyes as she pulled her lapa away from her thigh. I saw the big bone, completely broken, sticking out through the ruptured flesh and blood. In panic I ran down the hill towards the farm. It was an impulsive flight reaction. I ran almost all the way, until I met my parents at the farm. I tried to describe what I had seen but could not find the words.

On our return home, we saw Atekhai was busy, with people from the village working at the accident scene. The woman I saw had been removed from the spot under the tree. There were some people standing around, while others were busy in the area down at the creek.

Over six died in the accident and many were injured. It was said that the driver of the Bedford lorry lost control near the hilltop and galloped down through bush to the mine area, where the truck crash-landed in the creek at the bottom. I believe it was a miracle people survived.

The weeks turned into years, but I remain afraid of the unseen forces at Atekhai, especially the haunting eyes of that woman to whom I should have rendered first aid or stayed to comfort her in her distress.

A few years later, when I was in high school, I was going in the opposite direction, returning home from the farm with a group of friends. I heard that same woman recounting her story about the terrible accident, and she pulled up her lapa as if to reveal the scar on her thigh. She did not know that I was the little boy who had run away at the sight of the bone sticking out of her thigh.

Before the war that changed everything, I had only ridden in a car once—I thought that ride was quite a pleasure. It was during our return trip from the farm that the Peugeot 404 stopped to give us a ride. There must have been up to eight of us boys, and we piled one on top of the other. As the smallest, I sat on someone and could only see out the side window. I saw the trees along the roadside coming towards us, and I closed my eyes tightly until I arrived at home in order to avoid seeing the collision of car and trees.

Then we were warned not get into any cars with strangers—called *Igbomo-bgomo*—because they would kidnap children. Although we followed the instructions, we wanted to know more.

"What do they do with boys?" I asked

"The kidnapped children are sold to rich men who use them to make money. Once the child's name is called, the money will come in, as much as the man wants."

I was made to believe that some of the rich men have big stomachs because they have swallowed the pot of voodoo to make money. I was scared and had a keen scene of awareness that I didn't live in the city where many of the rich people lived.

One Sunday morning five of us boys were sent to the farm to bring bamboo back to the house for the garden fence. It was eerily quiet because it was Sunday, and the Ivbie were not walking to the market. We were halfway up the hill at Atekhai when a white Volkswagen Beetle, which was travelling in the opposite direction, appeared to stall then slow down to complete stop as it reached us. We saw the windows were rolled down. It was our signal to run.

I let go of my load of bamboo and ran along the footpath as an escape route through Ederuae to return home.

"Where is the bamboo? What is it that chased you out of the farm?" I was asked when I got home.

"Someone wanted to kidnap us."

One of the bigger boys walked us back to the farm. Halfway there we saw the same car returning, so we sneaked behind the big boy, who talked to the driver and then informed us it was nothing to worry about.

In similar manner like the pottery ventures of Ivbie, many have long abandoned the traditional wines (made from corn) and refreshing drinks passed on from one generation to the next. The natural, traditional drinks have been replaced by whiskey and sweetened soft drinks called soda or pop.

One could say that as the "civilized American" I am—and because of my presence in the U.S.—I became addicted to the sugary stuff. But I kicked the habit a long time ago when I realized the drinks were poison to the human body. Now and then, I do reminisce about the taste of some of the peculiar, locally brewed beverages of my home. One drink—my father called it Oburukutu—is a mild wine that was occasionally brought from the city when members of the village returned home.

Another one of my episodic reminiscences—I often find myself in peculiar situations—occurred as I was eating a crunchy pear one day. I was musing about its coarse-smooth taste when I remembered the distinct smooth-like taste of an Oburukutu. I went on the web to Google the word. I found its real name of Burukutu. I was excited and shared my rediscovery with my colleagues Rodney Morrison and Sarah Carmichael. I told them about the remarkable African Burukutu that comes in soft drinks, wine, or alcoholic beverages. My colleagues were intrigued by the existence of such beverages, but I cautioned them in sort of a disappointment that Burukutu was not yet available in the

U. S. However, it is still readily found throughout Africa, since it has continued to be brewed throughout the ages as a rich source of vital nutrients.

Rodney said, "One can make wine. It is not against the law to share with family and friends."

Is he serious? I thought, since Rodney has always teased me.

"You can make wine for personal consumption, and as long as it is not for sale, you don't need a license," Sarah confirmed.

I said, "I could make the Burukutu drink, but I do not think I will do so anytime soon. I would prefer to bring a few bottles back when next I travel to Nigeria."

Sarah was more emphatic. "You bring the wine from home for me!"

Despite efforts, whether intentioned or otherwise, to rid us of such traditional flavors, the modern world is recreating what was old as new again and seems to be holding onto the old, natural tastes. We have come to realize that people have forgotten the old tastes. The healthy claims of organic foods have been gaining ground, while others argue in favor of genetically engineered foods. Such situations have thus far epitomized the need to restore disappearing, traditional things such as the foods my father grew on our farm. I for one long for the unforgettable taste of Burukutu, which is the beverage similar to the one my father shared with us.

Chapter 13

Changing Times of Ye Khee People

The cultural changes after the Biafra War were similar in magnitude to the Empire revolutions we studied in secondary school. Little did I realize that I was partaking in the experiment!

There were no street names, only names of quarters at Afowa, but during the time I was in high school, the need to start naming the streets was realized and the Akhamie compound was recognized as a street:

Street	Quarter	Village	Clan	Ethnicity	Tribe
Akhamie	Uguolomi	Afowa	Uzairue	Etsako	Edo

Akhamie Compound Address

The *name* of anything was an important trait of our culture. The people have a saying that a frog does not run in daytime. Many times I saw the frog running, and the next thing I saw was a big snake.

By historical accounts, the tradition of creating the gap between the front teeth was considered to be charming, for its virtue, beauty, and welcoming smile. Only the wealthy and royalty could afford the cost of surgery. The elders accorded the split in the front teeth as virtuous and a sign of purity for the women who maintained virginity prior to marriage.

There were many versions of the dialects from one clan to another, but one commonality prevailed in the Afemai preface to conversations with "Yekhee" or "I say," so the people called it "Ye khaei."

As a scholar of Afemai literature, I came across a scholastic study of our dialects conducted by UCLA—titled "A Tonal Grammar of Etsako," by Baruch Elimelech—which probed into the intricacies of native dialects and exposed unique inter-relations among the tongues, customs, traditions, and culture of the Afemai. Many such traditions have been discarded with the intermingling of the Afemai culture with Western ways.

New Era

The 1960s/1970s marked the end of the standard school. The educational system had regarded secondary school as the equivalent of college, but there was major restructuring after the Biafra War. The society yearned for the good things in life: paved roads, running water, electricity, and modern infrastructures.

The hiccups were great in regards to fewer numbers of secondary schools to accommodate those graduating from elementary schools. However, more problems awaited those of us who completed secondary school and had no future opportunities. There was a well-known slogan in those days that stated: "to keep Nigeria one is a task that must be done." The battle had been won for a united Nigeria, my state of Bendel was now called Edo State, and the local government for Etsako was headquartered at Auchi. But questions about the future remained in the midst of a developing nation with an insurmountable and persisting social crisis.

In secondary school I began with the idea that I was in college and that I was being geared to encounter real training—like in the battlefields—for academic challenges. Our student body was comprised of some of the best minds from the primary schools throughout Afemai and from all over Nigeria. My pursuit of college—as compared to teachers training—amounted to better and diverse opportunities. The competition for limited spots in the prestigious colleges often involved candidates vying for the few federal government colleges, which were located in the cities.

At Our Lady of Fatima Boys College, the standards were already established for academic distinctions in the arts, sciences, and sports. My school was renowned for producing students who achieved the highest academic achievements of straight As in the West African Examination Certificate program (WAEC). The students created a song in Esan dialect about the Afemai: *Uwi yome khai dey ikolegi okah ka gbe – eh*. This means, "My beloved one, do not fall (fail) because college is tough!"

In other words, the beloved child of my village must not fail because college was tough, tough, and tough. The song was featured during sporting events as the students cheered somersaults and flipovers with two legs or danced the butterfly on one leg. Since the song was in the native dialect, it was discouraged as a sanctioned cheer or slogan, and it was reserved for use within the school campus.

My time at school seemed to fly by in a similar manner as the cultural edifications that swept through Afemai and the nation.

The principal of Our Lady of Fatima Boys College when I started form (class) one in 1973 was Mr. Patrick Iguonobe, a native of Esan (Ishan). Mr. Iguonobe was one of the first Nigerians to take over from the European missionaries who established the school in 1960. Students were from different parts of Afemai. We did not speak one dialect and could not communicate fluently in English. Pidgin was predominantly used, but English was mandated in the classrooms, which resulted in inevitable discipline for violating rules when we used Pidgin during class.

As day students, we returned home each day after classes. Some of us were not able to afford the extra cost of boarding, as our families were already making financial sacrifices to pay the school fees. The day students were seen as not participating in the school's social activities and carried the blame for the diminishing prestige of the college's status. The students came from the surrounding villages, had never traveled to a city beyond Auchi, were paying lower tuitions, and were not burdened with the extracurricular activities. Day students were accepted in the school community with reluctance, and resentment persisted in some instances until the students entered the school's hostel in the final two years, forms four and five.

For every student the obvious goal was getting an education, as it was the ticket to a better life. As such, the race started from the day one stepped foot onto the Fatima College campus as a student. The pressure to do well was real. Poor performance resulted in repeating the class or expulsion if the student's grades were not adequate. I was fortunate. I thank God for the blessings He gave me: I passed all my examinations and ranked in the top ten percent of my class, starting in the second year.

The social changes that swept through the country disrupted the emerging educational system still in its infancy, and it succumbed to mediocrity. By the end of my fifth year, in 1978, the secondary schools were no longer considered to be the equivalent of college but simply met normal international standards. Referring to our secondary schools as colleges was no longer applicable, and the name of Our Lady of Fatima Boys College was changed to Otaru Boys Grammar School. Years later, after I graduated from secondary school, the name reverted to the original "Our Lady of Fatima" name.

The syllabus for secondary schools across Nigeria was uniform because of the complete break from elementary school. The elementary schools taught arithmetic, English (its vernacular form), and social studies. There was an ethnocentric reliance on folklore in literature. The folktales with their lessons of famines and a thriving local economy were not taught in the high schools, which used a model based on English culture.

Europe-centric material in English test questions—such as to select the word closest to "white" from choices (a) cotton, (b) snow, etc.—bewildered us; we had never seen snow before. I recall the efforts of our English teacher, Mr. Ekhata, who provided a selection of idioms based on African frame of reference each week. One of idioms was, "I cried that I have no shoes to wear, but it dawned on me that I was blessed when I saw a man without a foot."

I was good at memorization, so I committed the idioms to memory and was disappointed when Mr. Ekhata withdrew his promised scholarly efforts. He scolded the class for a lack of interest and low participation. But I wish he had continued as, at that age, our minds were ready to absorb such concepts, even though not all of us committed them to memory. I related to the idiom regarding the "one without shoes," since it suited my own situation. I was still lacking many things, but I knew I was one of a privileged few who benefited from the opportunity to attend one of the better schools in Nigeria.

Good teachers were getting harder to find and retain since educated people joined in a host of nationwide transitions of one kind or another. The apparent shortage of teachers led to reliance on foreign teachers who came for one or two years from Canada, the United States, Pakistan, India, Egypt, and other places. The influence of the teachers was remarkable in preparing us for the future.

Through education at Fatima, I understood the concept of sacrifice some families made to send their children to my school. I became more studious in my efforts and worked hard in learning English. After each day's instructions, I would resort to memorizing idioms, words, and concepts. In the company of other students, I would try to rehearse and commit words to memory.

The art of memorization was a technique that many of us learned to cope when face with challenges, and it was reinforced by my English teacher, Mr. Ekhata, He told us, "Interest and enthusiasm are the ingredients of human endeavors." By the fourth year, I realized that my life was based on my willingness to own up to my challenges squarely by myself, and I was hardened by the struggle.

Every school day I walked the six miles. I would leave my house in the Oguolomi quarter at about 6:00 a.m., walk through my village, passing the old Demonstration Primary School, St. Angela Girls School campus and Notre Dame Hospital, walk straight through the town of Jattu, along the main road, passing the Hausa-Iyoruwa quarters and the Uzairue Market, and finally down the hill to Our Lady of Fatima, located in the valley. Along the way, walking briskly in the cold mornings, I met groups of students wearing the white-on-navy-blue school uniforms. This journey was repeated in reverse on the way back home each evening.

It was seen as "cool" for guys to have popular nicknames. The popular senior guy names in my first year were SOCO for Cyril Akhainemhe, Bulerasco, Tseseboyo, Kizito, Alumbe (Albert Agunu), Caterburi, Molarsco, and others. I could not come up with a catchy name. I tried the name Zapele—which sounds like Sapele, the name of a town—but it was not a good idea.

During the end of the second and third year at Our Lady of Fatima, I was in the role of a senior student along with my colleagues; Bruno Oshionebo and Anthony Agunu who were in the class ahead of me. I joined in the study groups of inductees called *awokos* (meaning staying up all night for cramming before the examinations). Anthony Agunu, Karimu Momoh, Dominic of Apana, Anthony Iluore and Anthony Ogbhemhe were among the group of day students who walked from Afowa to attend secondary school at Auchi. Anthony Iluore from Iyora was my classmate and stayed at our house where he often shared a room with Philip during the school sessions and returned home at Iyora on weekend as holidays.

David Akhamie and Our Lady of Fatima Boys Grammar School friends, posted at the Notre Dmae Hospital Uzairue

At Our Lady of Fatima, the students were engaged in rigorous academic competition to keep up with the classmates and maintain excellent grades. The top students resorted to constant studying to maintain their positions as smartest students. The training and education we received at the village set us on the path to great successful lives; by the times I left the village and lived in the United States;

Bruno Oshionebo became a medical doctor later established the first private modern health care at the Afowa; Anthony Agunu became a director at the National Biosafety Management Agency of Nigeria, Karimu Momoh became a Professor; and Anthony Iluore became an administrator and the list of successful men extended onto various high positions and places around the world.

Chapter 14

The First Encounter

Learning English was a huge task since majority of the students spoke only the native dialects. The limited exposure to English at school was desirable since there were no English speakers in our villages. There was no instruction in our native cultures. I was about 11 years old during my first year of high school. Upon returning from school early one Friday afternoon, I decided to visit my sister's house. It was about 4:30 p.m. Everywhere seemed deserted, but I failed to realize the students were still in their classrooms for the afternoon session at St. Angela Girls School. By the time I walked halfway across the campus, girls had started to come out of their classrooms and were going toward their assembly ground. Since I had already walked so far, I continued to move forward, hoping I could sneak through the broken fence in the area around the science building. I always avoided the main gate because there was a security guard on duty.

It seemed that I was surrounded on all sides. I kept walking and became keenly aware of the staring eyes; however, none of the all-female students stopped me. I walked right in front of the Sister, who said something to me. I knew I must say something in response, like polite people do. "Es ye-es, Sister," I said.

Frustrated by the absence of any substance in our exchange, the Sister said something like, "Sches... eces... and eses..." The message was, "Turn around and leave the way you came!"

Whether or not the posted signs warned against trespassing didn't matter, as I could not read them, anyway. However, I was ashamed since I was wearing the banana-yellow house uniform issued to the day students attending Our Lady of Fatima. I felt that I had presented a bad image of my school. In spite of the moment of embarrassment, I was inwardly glad that I did not get into serious trouble beyond that dreadful encounter at St. Angela Girls Grammar School.

Izobo, Osu, and Voodoo

In the rapidly evolving society, things that we were accustomed to were discounted in the schools. Here, a philosophical exercise would suffice as I raise the issue of words such as sacrifice, which to us means Izobo. Sacrifice is also voodoo, but the question then becomes, "What is sacrifice?" A good topic for an essay, maybe!

The Anglo-centric method is to begin with a dictionary meaning, but that totally dodges the real meaning of the word "sacrifice" in our ethnic reference of Izobo. In the same way, all aspects of our life were impacted. Whether it is positive or negative is an issue of individual judgment. As everyone has come to realize, many African names were based on traditions. One of my classmates was called "Izobo."

Since our school courses did not focus on such subjects, we were left to make sense of culturally significant matters on our own. As such, we missed unique opportunities of identifying who we were and the history behind our names.

We took upon ourselves the seemingly easy path of adopting Westernized names. Native names were not safe from the exploitation, as the Etsako name of Otsu was misconstrued as the Ibo cast of Osu after we read Chinua Achebe's *No Longer at Ease*. It matters that education nurtures the fundamental basis of a culture. Native cultures supply treasure troves of ways of life; however, lack of insight in developing those fundamentals robs the foundation of nativism. Instead, the rush was for easy routes to rid ourselves of anything deemed uncivilized, but in the process, that resulted in the unanticipated degradation of centuries of human advancements.

After many years of education and practical life experiences as an elder, I realized that the confusion of such words as "Sacrifice/Izobo" is universal.

In the Etsako dialect, Izobo surpassed the word "love," since love is a concept of the mind. The word "sacrifice" is reference in some regards to the parent who loves the child and performs Izobo. Sacrifice for one's nation, people, clan, state, or society, etc. is a course for betterment of humanity. The ultimate is sacrifice to a nation, as recognized in the honoring of those American "Gold Star" families. (In January 2005, the Gold Star Families for Peace (GSFP) organization was founded to recognize those who lost family members in the Iraq War. They are entitled to display a Gold Star in their windows or on their homes.)

About halfway through high school, I began to want to do better, although I did not foresee where my education would take me. I was beginning to read better, but during the third year I encountered another challenging curve ball. In addition to the nine basic subjects in years one and two, we were introduced to two new subjects: General Science—divided into Biology, Chemistry, and Physics—and Agricultural Science. We ended up with about fourteen subjects in that academic year; thereafter, students were expected to select their area of preference, either Science or Liberal Arts.

I perceived a superstition that some of the more brilliant students must have received unknown powers. Hearing rumors that the smartest students were fortified with voodoo power, I decided I needed to also have such a thing. I did not discuss this with my mother, because I knew she would not go for voodoo as help for me to cope with schoolwork. Neither would my father, who had mastered the art of self-reliance. Besides, my schooling was the responsibility of my senior brother. An easy way to get the voodoo was to go to my mother's cousin Uncle Dirisu at Okpella. Mother talked about him as being a medicine man, so I asked him to equip me with the extra magical power to be top of my class. I did not disclose my plan to anyone, not even to Uncle Sunday, who I could always count on for money.

On a Friday after school, with the little I was able to raise from my mother, I set out for Okpella. I sensed that my actions were in defiance of my father's rules, since he did not want us to be exposed to anyone apart from our siblings. I received support of my mother, who assured me that nothing bad would befall me. My first stop at Okpella was at Uncle Dirisu's house at Okugbe. I met Uncle Dirisu and his family, who were very happy to see me. It was the first time that I had visited Okpella, and I was struck by Dirisu's close facial resemblance to my mother. I told him why I had come, that I wanted something to help me do extra well in school. I did not ask him to conjure witchcraft, but I wanted a quick fix to make me smart.

In spite of a slight difference in the semantics of the Okpella dialect, we talked—but whether he understood everything or not was another matter. I told Uncle Dirisu that I needed extra help to pass my examinations and to be the top in my class.

I was in a hurry because I would have to go over to Uncle Sunday's after my visit with Uncle Dirisu. In the traditional ways, Uncle Dirisu said prayers of blessings and then went to the back of his house. He returned with a small wrapped packet containing a fine-grain mixture of sand. He said, "Take the sack with you to school and throw a little pinch of the grains over your shoulders before the beginning of each examination."

I said goodbye to those at Dirisu's household and continued on the walk of about twenty minutes to Uncle Sunday's at Ido. It was joyous seeing Uncle Sunday, who had returned from the farm. We had some pounded yams and bitter-leaf soup prepared by Rose's mother, Uncle Sunday's first wife. I did not tell him what had caused my short visit, as he was just elated to see me. He gave me more than enough money for my trip home. As night was fast approaching, I walked toward the Auchi-Okene road and waved at a taxi to go back to Jattu. I was able to flag one down going my way, which was quite a relief.

The dramatic turn of events on that trip went even crazier in the taxi. It was operated by Alacrity, and he was accompanied by one of the St. Angela female students from Auchi. I had always liked the girl, who was remarkably beautiful, and had thought of writing her a letter asking her to be my girlfriend. I decided on the idea of writing to her once I realized that she was in a league beyond my reach.

The experience at Dirisu's household conflicted with my instincts about the charms. At Afowa, many or almost every young person was enrolled in school, but no one attended school at Dirisu's house. The affluence of my father's household was notable, as seen in my native name of Ekhalewe, meaning "greatness in not hidden." Therefore, my stunt of seeking voodoo from a place with far less education, and traveling instead of studying, was irresponsible. I decided to hunker down. However, I had lost valuable time.

In a desperate effort I decided to cheat in History. I copied material from my notes. The examination began during the last period, so I went to a secluded area after lunch break to retrieve the copied material I had written on the foolscap (blue book) examination paper. I came into History class a little bit late to avoid inspection. As luck would have it, the copied material was a question on the test; however, my nervous shuffling of paper caught the examiner's attention. The teacher came over to my desk and looked through the copied material. That was my first and last attempt at exam cheating!

The end of the school year spared me further embarrassment with the assured promotion to class four and a passing grade in History. I learned the hard lesson that I needed to work hard at studying, not take things for granted based on certain dogmas which embolden the undesirable spirits of superstition and rob one of creativity. Mama's words had come full circle: "Hard work does not kill."

Chapter 15

Enlightenment

Over the years I have gone through formative changes in my personal character. I believed that life was good but like in the native song, "He who has life must live to the fullest." I engaged life in a determined manner, with a humble smile and mild manners. Always approachable, I strived to overcome emotional shyness and to be more accepting of people as they were. But I remained sensitive regarding failure. The years in secondary school enlightened me to the ways of the oyibos (white people) and other cultures. I was irreconcilable at the time because my parents could not pay my way through high school. However, their words of advice became my refuge. "I will have to make it through hard work," I kept saying to myself. "Hard work will not kill me; and I will not die when I fight back." Such expressions were based mostly on their own life experiences, and they always reinforced that hard work will not kill anyone.

How about courage, one might ask? I decided to face obstacles which had drawn my attention for a very long time. One of the obstacles was the huge locust bean tree that I saw from the road in the vicinity of the Ugholomi stream. Every year I saw the fruit of the locust bean tree was ready for harvest. Every season I was taunted with thoughts of climbing the tree to harvest the bean. I didn't matter whether I needed the bean or would sell it to make money; it was just to prove a point to myself as a stubborn adolescent.

The time came when I felt I could do anything I wanted as a grown man. After all, the locust bean trees growing in the wild didn't belong to anyone. Early one morning before sunrise, I made my way towards the meadows of Iyhadi (*okho toime*), machete in hand. As I walked through the woods and came closer to the tree, I noticed it was bigger than it appeared from the distance. It was at least 60 feet tall, and I couldn't wrap my hands around the trunk in a bear hug to climb it. The obvious question I asked myself was, "After coming prepared to climb the tree, do I accept defeat?" Almost in a whisper, I said, "I must do it today."

I made a few cuts for support and heaved up and up to the branches over 50 feet above the ground. Another challenge arose since I couldn't pluck the strings of beans hanging from the branches. Intuitively, I began cutting and chopping away at the branches, which snapped and, due to gravity, fell swiftly, crashing to the ground. The noise echoed in the distance.

I was exhausted. I looked around, and at the junction in the road, I saw my mother, accompanied by Mama Alege (Patrick, the other Alege). I had proved to myself that I could climb that tree and pluck the tantalizing beans, so I climbed down to the ground. I was relieved and continued on my trip to the farm.

When I arrived at the farm, I informed Mother about the locust beans, which I had gathered in a pile. She said, "I was concerned for the person who climbed to the top of that tree. I did not know it was you." Mama stayed calm but didn't say my names of praise, because she knew that any mishap could have proved fatal. But she knew that a child has to learn and grow; it was impossible to keep me under her bosom. Such was every mother's worry that she must keep her child safe. Like the mother eagle's act of throwing babies out of the nest, it should be of comfort for mothers/parents to know they have raised children who can soar.

Miracle of Learning

The miracle of learning happened for me every day at school. However, as I prepared for the finals and the West African School Certificate Examination (WASCE), I became entangled in the midst of disciplinary problems with the principal, Mr. Patrick Onwudili, and one of my classmates. At the beginning of the school year, Mr. Onwudili had issued new policies for the admission of day students to the boarding house. The change of policy seemingly denying boarding for seniors caused rumors that the principal was selling bed space to the highest bidders and admitting first year students by accepting bribes from their rich parents.

I was further dismayed when Mr. Onwudili imposed stricter rules for the senior day students that said they must vacate the hostel and apply for re-admission. We ignored the orders until Mr. Onwudili finally decided to enforce his new policies;

I was awakened about midnight by a flashlight shining on my face. I was totally disoriented as I tried to get on my feet, and my shorts must have fallen off. I tried holding up my pants, which slipped again, and I fumbled with my shorts until the group left me and moved on to the next student. I felt humiliated as I came outside the dormitory. I joined the other students in a shouting demonstration as we walked to Otaru's palace to register a complaint against the principal.

An omen of the hint our educational system was in an abysmal decline was the changing of the school's name from Our Lady of Fatima Boys College to Otaru Grammar School. The Board of Education did not have teachers and managers to operate the schools. Everyone adapted to the idea that the inescapable forces of corruption, nepotism, selfishness, and ignorance were beginning to shape the nation's schools. Our impressionable minds were led astray as we saw such corruptive motives; an indicative hallmark was the unsupportive school principal with his new policy for the final year students.

Prior to Mr. Onwudili, the former principal was an aggressive Catholic priest called McIvor. He could not maintain a stable environment for the students. Father McIvor and Mr. Gregory Amunne, the vice principal, could not manage the students, and the drop in discipline was blamed on the senior students.

In my situation, I had been longing to stay in the boarding house ever since I started form one. I finally convinced my brother Paul to pay the extra fees from his meager wage as a school teacher, but I was denied access. The well-off parents had drivers to cater to their kids and drive them to school, but I would have to continue trekking as a day student. The gap between the rich and the not so well off was being defined in my mind. It seemed as if Mr. Onwudili was there in order to maintain the status quo.

A few days after the march to Otaru's compound, seniors students were threatening to riot and were shouting down the senior prefect. Although a brilliant student, the senior prefect did not have the skills to assume any control over the senior class. During the meeting with the principal to restore order, the senior prefect talked about grievances afflicting the senior students but failed to raise the issue of accommodating the day students in the hostel. I decided to confront the principal directly to make my own case.

I shouted at the principal, "You must admit the day students." Regrettably, my statement did not play well, although I did receive a few "yeses," in response to my plea. But I made a big mistake shouting at the principal.

His personal vendetta did not blind him to overlook my behavior; I was never allowed in the boarding house. Luckily, I was not suspended from school. However, my troubles continued after an argument and confrontation with my classmate.

Thaddeus always liked to tease, and we got into a fight about my pronunciation of "cooperation" during that inauspicious discord with the principal.

"You have to report to the principal's office," we were told.

We were summoned to the principal's office. I perceived the principal's grudges against me had blinded his senses of impartiality, and this was the opportunity he had been waiting for to impose corporal punishment. Mr. Onwudili had a black rubber pipe in his office, which he used to land several blows on my body. Corporal punishment was acceptable but not for senior students.

Despite the beating, I was comforted in the knowledge that I would be able to complete my examinations without an expulsion. Mr. Onwudili instituted a strict expulsion policy for senior students a few months after my dreadful encounter. My classmate John Okpoloko was expelled from school for a time, which hindered his final year's performance.

I was confused about the situation and decided that I had to rent a room at a house close to school. My decision was unwise since I didn't have the means to survive on my own; I could not pay the rent or cook my own food. I used a little kerosene stove, borrowed a spring bed, and brought cooking utensils from home. I stayed there for a few months before realizing it was not working out well. I had to give up the place before December and the end of first term (semester).

Both Paul and Baba had finally gotten around realizing that I was the only senior student in such a predicament. I went to my father and informed him, "Baba, the principal of my school does not allow me to stay at the student hostel. Could you solicit the help of Mr. Adimeh "Ogha" Imokhai, so that he can help to get me back into the hostel?"

Mr. Imokhai was the brother of the reigning chief, who was a retired health inspector. All my classmates, including Mr. Imokhai's son Alex Imokhai, had been staying in the hostel since starting class four the previous year. Mr. Imokhai went to talk with the principal on my behalf, but the principal remained steadfast and refused to allow me into the hostel.

My confidence dwindled throughout that most far-reaching final year of high school. I sat for the mock test and did not pass. The impact on me was to accept my situation, which I could not change. There is an old saying that, "one cannot fetch the water that was flown past." As an intuitive action, it became a good decision that I enrolled for the General Certificate of Examination (GCE), which was the equivalent of the General Education Diploma (GED) in the United States. I also enrolled for all eight subjects I was taking. In May/June of 1988, I completed the finals, administered by the West African Examination Council (WAEC), and continued to prepare for the GCE, which came in December. I passed the finals and came in at division three, which was the same level as my classmates from Uzairue. None of us made division one or two that year.

I felt that my family was not so poor that someone couldn't step up to ensure that I stayed in the hostel when my colleagues left me at home during those final years four and five of secondary school. It was those life lessons which I disliked. However, Baba and Mama had remained steadfast on their resolve. "You can't blame anyone. You must make do on your own," I was told. In a roundabout way I was beginning to understand those things,

"You are a man. I have done my duties. So you must carry on and be man of your own! The school and the teachers will teach what is needed to pass or fail. That is it!" Baba said.

The Few Opportunities

Aneke Cecilia, my sister, lived in Benin City, and I decided to visit her and her family. The plan worked out well, since John Okpoloko and I had become friends. John was a city-smart student who resided in the hostel but was running into trouble during our senior year in high school. He could speak better English than most of us, so he talked a lot. The students nicknamed him "Kapuepue." I discovered that John had relatives at Benin City, so I decided to venture into the big city and entrusted him to assist me in getting to my sister's place. In my first adventure, John was taking me under his tutelage as the one who knew the way.

The trip began at Auchi Motor Park and we boarded a Peugeot 504 station wagon for the one hour to drive to the New Benin Motor Park.

John estimated as we boarded the taxi, "It takes about an hour to reach New Benin."

I asked John, "Why do they call it New Benin?"

John did not answer my question but told me that, from his estimation, my sister's address of Guobadia was in the New Benin area.

We arrived at the city of New Benin via Ikpoba Hill and went to our final destination at the New Benin Motor Park. We exited the taxi and were swallowed up in a crowd of people. In a matter of seemingly seconds, I was exposed to four-way intersections and traffic lights. Although the traffic lights were working, it seemed cars and pedestrians were crossing at will faster than my senses could grasp.

John had crossed the four lanes to the other side of the road. I was scared and did not move fast enough to stay with him. Things were moving so fast that I just wasn't prepared for such a moment.

The light turns red, yellow, and green. The cars, buses, and taxis wouldn't let the pedestrians cross the road when the light turned green. Everyone simply ignored the street light as if it were not there to control traffic. John called for me to wait and said he would come back to where I was transfixed in place.

After several failed attempts, I decided that I had had enough of the mess! I started to walk, almost running, but I heard the squealing noise of car brakes and the city taxi drivers screaming and cursing, "Bush boy!"

Chapter 16

The Enterprise Called Allah Dey!

The elders did not forsake the traditions outright, but they embraced many of the changes as the way to raise their children and to pass their heritage to the next and future generations. In furtherance of their efforts, the young boys, especially those seen as unfit to handle the rough-and-tumble, laborious life of farming, were allowed to attend school.

Baba decided that one of his older sons, Albert Umoru, was the one who would spearhead the newly found quest for Western education. Albert was one of the first in the village to attend the standard school. As a young man and upon completion of standard school, Albert also became one of the first who went to Lagos, where he stayed to raise his family until he passed away in 2008.

Despite Baba's intuition to stake the future of his family on the potential of Western education—which he realized as the wave of the future—things did not work as envisioned. However, in his own way he had planned for his sons by ensuring they had opportunities to attend school and to go further to the university.

Father, along with the elders, was able to share the profit from the transportation corporation with stock options and dividends based on the investment of each household. The company was a remarkable achievement, since none of the owners had any formal education, but it was able to expand and gain prominence throughout the nation.

The story was told that during the planning stage to build the corporation, the elders were called to a discussion at the palace. The chief and elders listened to the ideas of the learned men about the idea of working together as a group to leverage resources, and they agreed every family would have an equal opportunity to invest. The profits would then be distributed according the shares owned by each family.

The elders decided the transportation company would operate under the slogan of "Allah Dey," as opposed to the village name of Afowa-Uzairue. Signs reading "Allah Dey" were visibly displayed on the front and backs of the trucks. The reasoning for using Allah Dey was probably a ploy to pacify the northerners and Hausas from any hostility toward the company. The trucks and trailers operated between Uzairue and places as far as Kano and Sokoto.

My father was the treasurer, and many of their meetings were held at our house. The educated males of Afowa, who were appointed as bookkeepers and accountants, were very frequently at our house to conduct transactions. Sometimes, there were bundles and bundles of money to be counted, and between the trips, my father would spread the money during sunny days to dry. The company remained profitable throughout the '60s and into the '70s, which was when the people in the village got the idea that my father was so rich he had to spread his money in the sun to dry.

During the annual stockholders' meetings, which every stockholder usually attended, the dividends were divided and given as cash to each stockholder. I enjoyed the moments, since the food was prepared by my mother, which meant there would be more meat. Occasionally, I was among those who did the butchering, and I would receive extra, fresh fat to roast in the open fire.

As usual, and as was expected, some "naysayers" predicted the business would not return any profits. At one of the meetings, one of the well-off families gave the excuse that, "We cannot part with our money if we do not have the know-how to operate a corporation."

They had gone to consult the oracle, which predicted that the business was going to fail. The message came from the head of the well-off family. He said, "We want a refund of the money we invested. The oracle told us the business venture was not going to succeed."

It was a scary proposition for the elders, but Afowa took a leadership role in support of education, trusting that the educated sons would come home with good ideas. They went on with the corporation and the support of education, which did produce many educated young men. Some of the young men were recruited to manage the bourgeoning businesses. Some were career employees, who went to live in the city, working for the corporation. Later, some established their own businesses. In a sense, the ambitions of our elders became the motivator for many of the young men of the village to start their own entrepreneurial ventures.

No other village within the Uzairue clan followed the vision of the Afowa elders, who were not going to be deterred during some of the downturns and crises of business operations. The majority of the village elders, like my father, were not going to be held back, either by the vestiges of or reliance on superstitions, nor the "never-do-well" attitude of some. They were unified in their collective efforts in championing advancement to elevate the status of Afowa.

Allah Dey was the pride of the village because it stood firmly as a thriving business during the Biafra War era. The pride was truly evidenced, especially on market days, when the villagers rode on an Allah Dey vehicle to the Uzairue market.

The women were assisted in getting up the ladder to the back of the truck. For the young men, there was a special style of slapping the board and leaping, hanging onto the ladder with one hand while one leg hurdled along. The bigger boys would have to demonstrate their skills at climbing atop the loaded trailers.

One of the managers was nicknamed Overload. Everywhere he went in the village, his praises followed. Arrival of the huge trucks was always a jubilant event with everyone shouting, "Allah Dey! Allah Dey!" Everyone welcomed the drivers as they parked in the village square and in other open areas.

The Biafra War constrained businesses as well as everyday activities; however, the business venture aspirations of the village continued to prosper. The war placed many things in chaos; it was a different time which presented its own challenges. In view of the tough times, we were told not to shout "Allah Dey" to signal the arrival of the trucks. When the military began commandeering trailers for the war effort, the elders held discussions about strategies to prevent the seizure of their trucks and trailers. It was decided to hide the trucks out of sight once they returned from their trips.

An all-out caution was put in place to lessen the shouts of "Allah Dey" and not discuss the whereabouts of the vehicles. The trailers were driven away—through the only street wide enough to allow passage—from the usual parking places at the village square to be hidden in the area around Imonigie's compound. The men climbed up the coconut trees and cut down palm leaves. The boys were called to gather the leaves and were assigned the task off covering the tire tracks. With branches of palm leaves, we went to work, chanting, "Voooh-ing" as we rode the imaginary vehicle of palm fronds, running from one end of the street to the other.

"Vu Voo Vooo," some other kids chanted, making the sound of the Mercedes tractor's big engine.

It was rather an entertaining episode for the boys to cover up the heavy tire tracks as we ran from one end of the street to the other. Within moments everyone joined in, as this was an enjoyable thing from which no one would be excluded.

I count myself as fortunate to have benefited from the aspirations of visionary elders who established modern business ventures, especially their strategies (i.e. objectives, plans, tactics, operations, managing, etc.). I realize that their dreams seemed insurmountable, but they passed onto to us those dreams of bigger things beyond their time. The naysayers' perceived obstacles prevented them from partaking in the unified undertakings of the village when they gave in to fear of the unknown. However, our parents took a firm stand, which made them the first to venture beyond subsistence farming, and thus gave us the biggest gift to be passed on to our future generations.

The corporation was big enough to accommodate any monetary contributions anyone in the village could afford, which was their strategy to negate anyone's excuses about not buying stocks or investing in the company.

During the reign of Chief Imogierua of Afowa; Akhamie and fathers; including Ogbhemhe, Diamisah, Imonigie (Salumo and Aghadabi), Uloko, Imokhai (Chief Imoghierua and Adimeh; Secretary), Ikhumetse, Umoru Agene, Adekulu (the washman), Oreghemhe and Sedunu; and many others, whose names have been registered in the ledger of Afowa Incorporated, were the pioneers who dared to invest in the venture. Then another group of men and the one that still thrived until they built a house in Afowa with their proceeds comprised of the following members:

> James Agene (*the only one living at the writing of this story*)
>
> Damisah Okpafi
>
> Matthew Okhukpe
>
> Jimoh (Gima) Ikhumetse
>
> Amedu Ikhumetse
>
> Momoh Enaboagah Ikhumetse

Basil Ogbhemhe

Phillip Amedu Agene

Patrick Agadabi Imonigie

James Uloko

Anthony Sule Imokhai

Killian Gomina Omomoh

Matthias Akpaegboye Agunu

Egbeagonor Akhanemhe

Some received their head start in life, such as the benefits from the village business, scholarship, and ingenuity of pioneering the modern era. Originally, I thought their mindset was abandoning the village, thinking they were ignoring the people who set the foundation stone of the village. But I have since chosen to emulate the practice of my father's generation to look beyond the present to seek a future bright with opportunities.

"Life is sweet in Lagos," the people would say, the word "sweet" meaning the pleasurable lifestyle. I saved my share of the cash flow that was available in no other place but Lagos. My friend Sule—Suleiman Abdulmaliki, a co-worker—said, "We have to hustle. As Lagosians, we have been so broke, we know what it is to have no money in the pocket, so we must appreciate the real value of money at a youthful age. We must save as much as possible rather than spend it on parties with friends."

Sule was more outgoing than I, so we began to consider the idea of him going overseas. We met an Ibo student from the USA who helped with Sule's admission to Eastern Washington University in Cheney, Washington. We all worked together to get Sule to the United States.

Once he arrived at the university, he reciprocated by obtaining my admission and getting me to the U.S. as well.

I wanted to say to my father, "Baba, I have a lot of money now!" Of course, he would have looked at me like I was crazy because, according to the Afemai saying, which can be found in the song by Bolivia, "the mouth does not talk of the barn of maize, but rather one looks up to the roof." It means that the good farmer is judged by the size of his barn, not simply by his bragging talk. I could say, "Baba, I have made more money than I can spend," but he would not be impressed by such an extravagant display.

Baba and the other fathers at the village enjoyed smoking Henry Moore tobacco, which was not available in the villages. When Baba acquired some Henry Moore, he used it sparingly so it would last a long time. When it was running low, Baba would mix the Henry Moore with native tobacco. I thought to bring some along from Lagos when I visited home for the holidays. My idea worked well, and Baba certainly enjoyed the dozen packs of Henry Moore.

"Use it as much as you want! I will get you more," I assured him.

My joy was to see him splurge, and he called his best friend, Eramha Uloko, to share with him. On subsequent visits, I bought extra Henry Moore. The thing I wanted to tell Baba was that I was surely ready to go solo and wanted to get on with my adventures. I waited until one my last visits before I said, "Baba, I am going to study abroad at a university in America."

Father did not question my plans regarding how I was going to pay for my university education and take care of myself. We looked each other in the eye for a long moment. Not too many words were spoken! From the look in my father's eyes, I was sure he was confident that his dreams for me would be fulfilled. It was the last time I saw my father, Momoh Akhamie "Akhamiemona" Osigwe.

Chapter 17

Departure to the City

My departure from Afowa-Uzairue came just after I completed secondary school. I felt the time was overdue to move away from the village and home after experiencing a series of tough times. I could not find a job in the Etsako area, Auchi, Okpella, or even at Benin City, the capital city of Edo State—formerly known as Bendel State. Having nothing to do, I hung around with friends and schoolmates who were in the same situation. I left the village and stayed temporarily at Benin City with my sister Cecilia Aneke and her family.

My stay at Guobadia, New Benin, was short but offered brief relief from the boredoms at the village. The breadwinner, my sister's husband Eramha, was traveling to England for further education. "We're moving back home," Cecilia told me. "As you know, Eramha will be away for two years." My sister told me they would have to endure the changes from city life to village life. The turn of events appeared to put my situation into reverse.

Shortly thereafter, my sister and her children moved back to the village, which also resulted in my return to Afowa. By then it had been almost a full year since I left high school, and I tried to find another way out of the village. My options at the time involved staying with close family or with my siblings. I thought about many places to go, but ended up returning to Benin City, where I stayed with close relatives (family cousins).

"I will continue to search for a job," I informed our cousin Bernard "Rakindo" Ogbhemhe (BRO).

BRO's place in Uselu, Benin City, had two rooms and was fully occupied. Including BRO and his wife, his wife's niece and BRO's younger brother Christopher (now deceased) lived there.

"I did not know that Ben had married." I informed Christo.

"Oh, yes. And I have been staying here for a while now. The girl is the niece of my brother's wife and she is staying with us, too. She graduated from secondary school in Benin."

I met BRO's wife, who was a nurse and who was almost ready to have a baby. I felt it was a bold move to invite me to stay with them, given the situation, and without any prior notice. I felt really awkward at first, which showed in my mood.

"Do not worry, come with me," Christo said, "I will show you the latrine and bathroom." We walked over to the end of the hallway in the two-story building. "We share these facilities with the other tenants. Use any of the bathrooms, it is first come first serve," Christopher advised me. "It is not a problem; those who are working leave early in the morning before those of us not working wake up."

Christopher was young and had an optimistic outlook on things. He was respectful to everyone, and for the two or three weeks I stayed there, we played music. Occasionally, the niece received visitors, one of whom brought disco music by Donna Summer. The visitors were about my age, but we basically ignored each other's presence and did not say much.

My stay with BRO and his family was short, but such welcome demonstrated the respect and beauty of African hospitality. Even though the cousins and nephews were much older, about the same age as my senior brothers, they did not ignore our relationship. BRO and others welcomed me to stay with them, as it is African tradition to look out for family.

As part of Akhamie's family, we are closely related as cousins to Ogbhemhe's family, and BRO is the firstborn of Mrs. Fanni and Obakhena (Basil) Ogbhemhe. At Afowa we maintained close friendships throughout our childhood and beyond. Because of the age differences, we regarded the older men as senior brothers. I was the same age as Ochuwa (a girl), who followed Fidelis. Philip was closer in age groups to Fidelis, but once Philip went to Lagos at a young age, I became close buddies with Fidelis (Achiza). During my final year in secondary school, Fidelis and his brothers joined their father's sawmill business at Jattu. The business site was not too far from my school. It was during my transient stays in Lagos, and we grew apart after that. I am not sure exactly when in 1983 we lost Fidelis due to an accident.

I was touched when I heard of Fidelis' death. Later on, Christopher also passed away. BRO's wife has also passed. At the time of writing this story, our parents have all passed on. With the passing of so many of the people I grew up with, my absence from home has truly compounded the loss.

The goodness of inclusion allowed every young person to experience life—some might call it happiness—in a shared environment. Each season had its joyous times, for instance, when the various holidays fell about the same period, as in the periods of the Muslims' Ramadan, or Eid al-Adha, and Christmas or New Year, or the traditional initiation ceremonies.

During the holidays, those who returned home after long absences would tour the village to meet and greet their uncles and aunts. The aunts would coddle the city people, holding them on their laps and carrying them as babies. The tradition of older women carrying the people who have been out of their lives for a long time is their way of reconnecting the child with the mothers who have departed.

I was fortunate to have known Ogbhemhe, who lived until about the same time as our grandmother (Uwewe) Okhee. As the senior or first child of his mother, Ogbhemhe was very close to Akhamie, and they worked together side by side as brothers.

Ogbhemhe was over six feet tall and was known as the village architect. One fascinating thing about him was the length of his feet: twelve inches. In measuring sizes for new buildings, there were no tapes to measure rooms of ten-by-ten feet. It was easy to count Ogbhemhe's steps—with his twelve-inch feet—and so he earned the title of architect.

Basil Obakhena Ogbhemhe's riches extended beyond the clan. He had made money from contracting business ventures going back to the era of the old Mid-Western Bendel State. The old pictures of him, which were taken with his European partners during the era, were displayed prominently on the walls of his living room.

As a main contributor to Afowa's transporting company, he also purchased his own private car and owned the heavy vehicles of our father's transportation ventures. While the Allah Dey lorries were parked at the village square, his were parked in front of our compound at Ogbhemhe's family house. One of his younger brothers, called Ayagbode, was a trained driver and he operated the transporter from Afowa to the east (Iboland) and throughout the northern parts (Hausa) of Nigeria. He purchased the tipper, which was used to supply gravel and the white sand from Atekha. Obakhena was also the main consultant for Afowa regarding the mining of the mineral deposits.

At the height of his business operations, his vehicle was seized because of the Biafra War, and that probably set in motion the downward trends that wrecked the lives of many in our village, which then rippled beyond. Obakhena later experienced the affliction of alcoholism for several years as his properties and businesses failed. The three wives and children at the house held together. However, the strain of alcoholism took its toll. Obakhena later recovered and was able to coach his children and to pass on the traditions of Ogbhemhe, who was known for his entrepreneurship.

As in the name of Afeakuna—which means that it is the family that one fights for—we have to follow the course of our elders in guarding the younger ones. An African proverb that says, "The youth can walk faster but the elder knows the road," reminds me there are many nearly forgotten stories that were passed down by our elders. Many of the people I knew as a child have passed on. Still, there are many inspiring hereditary traits that continue to prosper.

Akhamie, Ogbhemhe, and Idalu shared two separate compounds with a combined size of four acres. Akhamie's household covered the larger portion, and Ogbhemhe and Idalu stayed on the other side. The men in the families shared similar activities. The men also lived in the two-story main house with their young wives until they branched off on their own.

Throughout the years I often observed how meals, work, and other activities were exchanged. Those who attended school at the same time often shared many things. My senior brothers shared parallel lives with their cousins in the Ogbhemhe and Idalu households. Those who attended school likewise did things together during holidays. One of my brothers, Boniface Akhalume, who was nicknamed Iticha because he remained as the school teacher, was close in age to William Okhani Ogbhemhe, who went to college to study agriculture. While Okhani was at home, he worked closely with Boniface in raising ducks, guinea fowls, and all sorts of vegetables in the garden.

Boniface planted guava and cashew trees on the property close to the house. Okhani had a chicken nursery and eggs were sold to the surrounding institutions. Basil Obakhena Ogbhemhe was an industrialist, and one of the first in the village to have business relationships with white men. Obakhena set up a factory for producing rubber latex. In essence, the two compounds were the industrialized sections of the village.

Providing educational and career training for the children was a main goal of Father and his cousins. I must not forget to mention the women, of course. "Miss," the brilliant young wife of Jacob Idalu, was a delight during the time she stayed in the village.

In playful fashion, there were funny commotions between Idalu and Miss, his daughter-in-law. We were entertained or captivated with Idalu in his good moods. Idalu was the funniest person around, a world of difference from Akhamie and Ogbhemhe, who were more business minded. Miss's husband, Jacob Idalu, was a handsome man who pursued education to become a university graduate and one of the first from the village to become a school principal. When he retired, he became the chairman of the Etsako local government.

I have fond memories of the times spent together with Miss and Jacob's children, Valentine and Henry (Ferdinand was little at the time and did not come out to play with us). Not long thereafter, they moved away to the city.

The cousins' relationship had its roots through my grandmother Okhee, who lived to be the oldest person in the village—which would be above ninety—and we were delighted for her position of honor.

During celebrations and events such as funeral, the processions of music and dancers on parade had to stop at our compound to give gifts and compliments. They would play a couple of rounds as the ladies from the house stopped whatever they were doing to join in the dance. The eight oldest people in the village were celebrated with reverence, respect, and admiration for their wisdom, and people came by to receive prayers and blessings.

The daughters of both Akhamie and Ogbhemhe—her grandchildren—came regularly. On the way to see Uwewe, the women always stopped at my father's or came to my mother's quarters. I got to know a few of the older women. Two of the very close ones, Iyorefo and Imhono, were the siblings of Ogbhemhe and Idalu. Although confined to her quarters because of blindness and crippling arthritis,

Uwewe remained the powerhouse of love until she passed away in the early 1970s (i.e. about 1971).

My mother cared for my grandmother. Uwewe did not bath every day, and Mother was forbidden by tradition to give her baths. As a little boy, it was allowed for me or Philip to bathe her. When her health declined, we were not allowed to be too close to her. It was believed that old folks would take one of the children along to "carry the load" on the journey to the land of the dead. And when this happened, the child would die.

Most of our relatives came to take care of Uwewe. It is not fully clear how we were related. I did not know that the mother of Ogbhemhe, Idalu, and their sisters were related to my grandmother Uwewe; as nephews and nieces.As such, Ogbhemhe, Idalu, and their sister were our first cousins. Although the lineage was not well defined, everyone always believed as told that we are blood relatives and, as such, it was strictly forbidden to have romantic relationships with each other. It was a concern of the elders that we know who was related to whom, but they assumed that living together was enough to maintain the status quo of family.

However, with the death of many elders who had firsthand information of the relationship between the two families was lost. Peter, who has been working diligently with the elders, has established the ancestral linage to the ninth generation as illustrated:

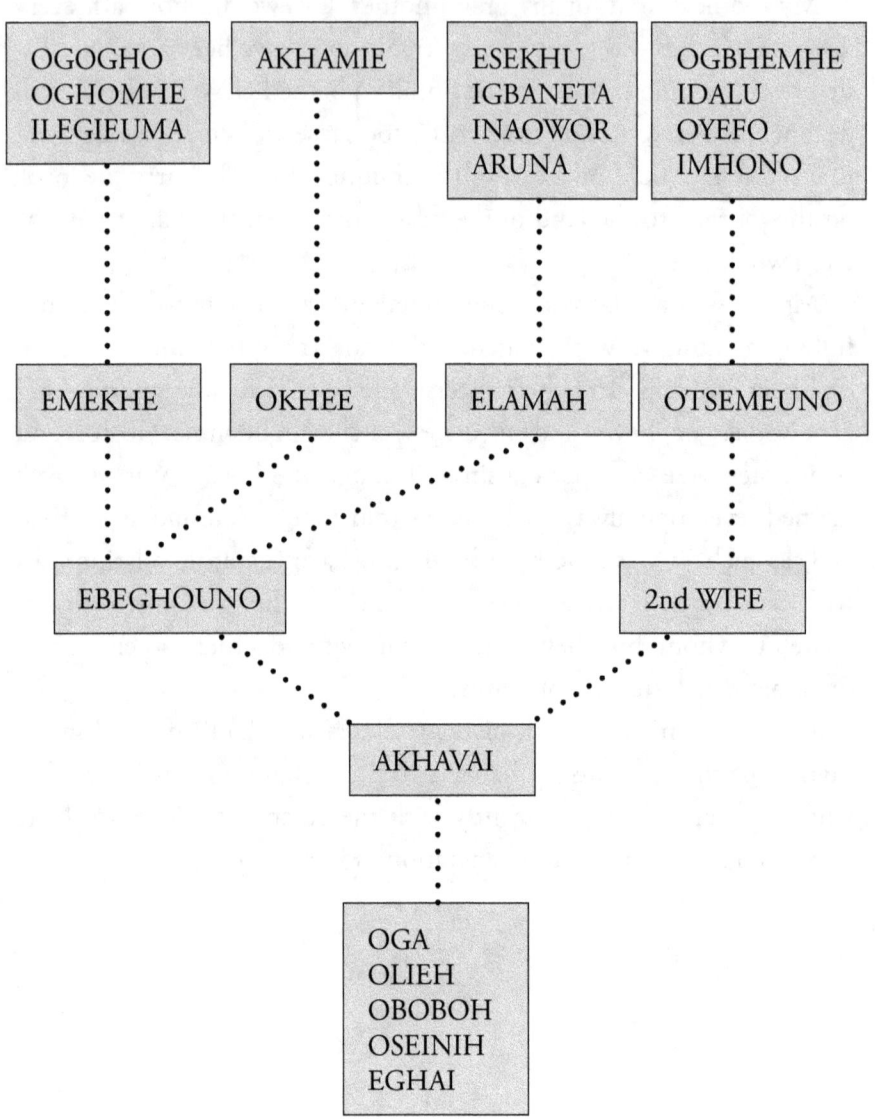

It has been determind through oral history that Oseinih was the distant patriarch of the Oghuolomi dynasty (quarters).

According to the elders, Akhavai was the father of Okhee, Emeke and Elamah and their mother was called Ebeghouno. They lost their parents while they were teenagers so Elamah Akhavai was responsible for them. Akhavai was also the father of Otsemouno who gave birth to Ogbhemhe, Idalu, Iyoefo, and Imhonu.Elamah, Okhee's senior brother, gave birth to Esheku (mother of Eragbe), Egbaneta, Inuawor, and Arunah (the handsome young man who died after marriage to the young bride called Isametu). Ismaetu was later married to my father Akhamie Osigwe.

In Afemai genealogy women are hardly mentioned since they are completely assimilated in their husband's family. Akhamie usual maternal family ties is understandable since his parent had to leave Uluoke, the paternal ancestral home, to settle at Afowa with the in-laws. Okhee's sisters Emeke was married in the village of Ayua, and gave birth to Ogogho, Oghomhe, and Ileghioma.

One thing that has been established about the relatives was that Akhamie (Okhee's son), and Otsemeno's children (Ogbhemhe, Idalu, Iyoefo, and Imhonu) were first cousins. My brothers and me followed in the same line of ancestry and the majority of Oghuolomi descendants are recognized as the great/great grandchildren of Otsinih, hence are forbidden from inter-marriages within Oghuolomi quarters.

Ogbhemhe Otsemeuno
First cousin of Akhamie Osigwe; the families lived on the expanse of compound as brothers with the young brother Idalu and their sister
Ogbhemhe passed on the tradition of entrepreneur to his offspring; from Basil Obakhena to the grandchildren. Among the grandchildren include Bernard Rakindo Ogbhemhe (BRO) who is a notable mathematician and engineer. His offspring have travelled to Europe and United States.

Idalu Otsemeuno

Idalu is second cousin and brother of Ogbhemhe. He travelled throughout the place as a performer making music and people happy. He had two wives and his children were among the first to graduate from the universities at Afowa. Jacob Idalu was a school principal and Chairman of Etsako local Government. His grandchildren have traveled to Europe and are making impacts.

David Akhamie

PART III

NIGERIAN MAN

One who is a Nigerian and who is willing to succeed and live life to the fullest as ordained by God. It is a belief we uphold dearly.

Chapter 18

Nigerian Man

After I graduated from secondary school at the age of seventeen, I began to face the stark realities of life. It was a period of chaos. It was much the same for my colleagues, since few of them had any plans either. My nephew Anthony (Tony) Akhamie came home, and we shared one of the rooms upstairs in the family house. Anthony landed a job as an elementary school teacher. He was lucky, as there weren't enough positions for every one of the recent graduates who applied for the few vacant teaching jobs at the elementary school. Anthony went to work; I continued trying to find a job within the local area. However, paying jobs became harder to find after all the teaching vacancies were filled.

My bright moment came following the release of the GCE results, which showed my remarkable improvement in six out of the eight subjects, a division one level if I passed mathematics and English. Compared with the WASC results, the GCE was an impressive Division One level. I was eternally glad I had retaken all the subjects I sat for during the previous WASCE. However, even though my results were above average, they were not good enough to secure my admission to the country's higher institutions of learning. Some of my mates returned to school for another year in order to retake the WASCE.

The country was unprepared to employ all the young people graduating from the different institutions. Everyone was left without any guarantees of employment, but they forged ahead just the same.

My hopeless situation hit home when I realized there was nothing to look forward to. "Maybe someone from within the family will come to my aid? Just maybe a nudge to help me," I said to Tony. But my words were met with deafening silence as no answers came from anyone anywhere. Day by day I became more disillusioned as I realized there was no need hanging around at the village, where I was becoming a burden to my parents.

Anthony Akhamie, Jerome Imonigie, and I stayed close together, and occasionally Fidelis (Achiza) Ogbhemhe and Braimah Dirusu, the Lagos boy, came to join us. We played card games at night and spent most days between the Akhamie and Imonigie compounds.

The close friends shared clothes to go out to parties. We shared novels and other books. Once novels were introduced into the circle of students, they were passed around from one person to another. Students from the neighboring villages of Afashio and Jattu exchanged American novels and magazines, and we read thrillers by authors like James Hadley Chase and Nick Carter.

Most of us had never been to the cinema, but we created our own imaginary realities, such as that we were from urban areas of America. Without any club anywhere nearby, even at Auchi, our entertainment was parties. We organized our parties at the villages and reserved a parlor in a house with enough space to accommodate many teenagers and a stereo for music. My problem was when it came the time to pay for my share of the costs. I did not have the money and there was no one to ask to pay for me.

A bigger problem was staying away from the dance, especially when I could hear the music blasting enticing tones. One night friends from another village came by and wanted me to escort them to the party.

Ashamed to admit that I had not paid, I went to the dance and managed one or two rounds before I was spotted:

One of the patrons issued a challenge. "David, what are you doing here?" Knowing that I must stop further accusations, I struck the guy, who was much bigger and stronger than me, and landed a blow.

I had started the fistfight and then I headed for the door, but he was much faster. He came after me, fought with me, and I fell hard on the ground. He was on top as older men came upon us and stopped him from landing more blows. It was an embarrassing mess-up, which was my fault. I just couldn't resist the temptation to crash my friend's party.

The long period of idleness lasted from 1988 into 1989. I exhausted all avenues of finding a job within the Etsako area. The next plan was to travel to Benin City and stay there with my sister to continue the job search. My stay in Benin City was short because I found the same situation there that I had left back home: a lack of employment opportunities. My sister returned to the village when her husband went to the United Kingdom for further studies in teaching.

How come my education seemed to have failed me in providing answers, I wondered. I searched for ways to reconcile traditional beliefs, superstitions, religion, and life in general. My solemn inner voice hinted at me to reflect on the motto of my village's primary school: "knowledge is power." It is a concept that has generated much debate over the years but could be refashioned as "knowledge is applied power."

I read that Francis Beacon, a British author, was the one who expressed the idea many years ago. Of course my immediate problem was how I could apply my education in the changing society. That was when the lessons of the village elders about not resorting to confrontation came into play. They trusted in the education system as the way of the future.

My education began at home, and I have many role models to look up to. The girls about my age were completing high school before getting married, and a few were receiving the financial support to go further to the teachers training colleges.

I listened to the stories within our house that my father was among the first in Etsako to embrace formal education by sending his sons to the standard school. He continued to push for his children to have a university education, but he had quieted somewhat by the time I went to high school, since he had left Paul in charge of me. For the most part he didn't pressure anymore like had when the villagers joined together in financing the education of the village's brilliant students, who were to bring good things back to the village when they attained important or powerful positions.

Along the way, my father and other elders realized the peculiar culture of Western education that mainly "preserved the individual," and as such it was the free will of the individual whether or not to share their knowledge. Much was therefore expected from those the village sponsored, but it was not reciprocated. In summing up the feelings of the village elders, Baba always used to say, "Some of the university graduates became rich because of their high positions in the country. We gave them scholarships to become pioneers, but they used their knowledge to pursue selfish goals. Everyone has to seek for themselves. We, the elders, are now resigned to the point of realism that education is one flying solo."

I experienced recurring dreams of learning to fly to escape from forces attempting to catch me. In real life I saw no way out, so I had dreams which assured me that I would "fly" and would overcome obstacles. I did not discuss those dreams with anyone. I relished the dreams that I would soar, but such a thing was taboo and seen as witchcraft. Many awful things were blamed on the witches, including deaths.

In the stories told, Witches operated in darkness and flew from their beds to faraway places but returned before dawn. They are able to travel beyond the seas to reach anyone they wanted to kill. The witches were known to gather at the top of huge trees, and some of the brave villagers who ventured out in the darkest of night have seen burning fires on tree tops and big campfires under the shade of huge trees.

From the time I was old enough to understand, the stories about witchcraft were inculcated in my psychic and caused fear. Because of the ignorance of others, I learned the bad superstitious beliefs, which preyed on my innocence. There was the death of the most educated young man of Afowa—he was a medical student—in America. He was a few years away from becoming a medical doctor, but the witches went there and killed him.

What about the ocean, one might wonder? On the three-day journey, the witches transformed into some small objects. The funeral was one of the saddest periods in the village, since someone who was in a position to change our lives had died.

The witches were rumored to be cannibals who fed on the person they killed. Such beliefs have never faded from our society. The educated ones were not spared. Some believed that secret societies such as Ugboni create wealth for its members, but the person would be killed eventually for his blood. A person may still be alive for a time after the witches have taken his blood, but sometime later he will die.

As such, when it came to flying, whether in a dream or as in the freedom of a spiritual being, it was nothing to tell anyone. It was also rumored that the witches would eat the parents of the person who gave someone up to the witches. It was payback for the witches eating another person's child. The logic of witches does not match real life, something that was not discussed in high school.

The things unknown which defy explanation were blamed on some evil spiritual forces such as witches and devils. During times of tragedy, victims went to voodoo priests (obos) to find answers. To be able to have purpose in one's life, one had to fight against forces in life in a constant struggle and not succumb to defeat of the ever-present but unseen forces, entities, and spirits. Through my adolescence and onward, I had been set on the idea that in life, whether in the village or elsewhere, I had to face so many things that I had to overcome.

Chapter 19

Trip to Eko, Lagos

At Benin I used to walk everywhere in the city and quickly came to know my way around. I went from New Benin to the major subdivisions of Uselu, Ekewa, Ikpeba, Sakpoba, and other parts. The daily conversations with people were exciting chances to speak Pidgin. Edo tribes had most of the spoken dialects in Nigeria, and the residents of Benin City had a different language from my native dialect. I was determined to practice saying the smoother tones like the city people, which was my other reason for going away to the city.

Back in the days at the village, my brother Peter had introduced me to the idea of writing to pen pals. Since about my second year in high school, I had maintained pen pals as friends. It was also a way of satisfying my curiosity as I tried to reach out to the world in Nigeria and beyond.

My first pen pal, Kiss Versluis, was from Holland, and we exchanged letters for about three years before we lost contact. Initially unsure of myself that I would write well enough for the white kid from Holland, I relied on my cousin Basil Idamisah, who was a senior at school, to help me. Later, I realized that it was a mistake; I should be writing on my own. It was good practice and would improve my writing skills. Shortly thereafter, family members began to come to my room to ask me to write or read letters for them. Such tasks of helping those who are illiterate were reserved for the educated like me.

At Benin City I yearned to resume my hobby of writing to pen pals, and I chose the United States in order to interact with the black youths about my age. I wrote to a few selected names which were published in the reigning black magazine, *Right On!* I did not receive any responses. I thought that those whose names were published in *Right On!* magazine may have received many letters and would not be able to respond to mine. I decided that I would have to try other ways. I felt like I had hit the jackpot when my name and picture were published in *Oh Boy*, one of the United Kingdom teenagers' magazines.

In my letter of request to the editor, I used the caption "Help" as a catchy attention getter, but I was unaware of what the results of that plea would be when the letter was published. Apparently, the idea of the caption was one of the lingering habits of the village mentality syndrome of forging ahead and feeling my way out as I transitioned to city life.

Whether it was a call for help or the widespread circulation of the magazine, a flood of letters came to P.O. Box 22, Afowa-Uzairue, within a month after I had left home in 1979. The letters that came from the United Kingdom were handed over to Anthony for safekeeping. I replied to the first wave of letters, but it soon became obvious that I would not be able to write to everyone. I decided to share the letters with mates at Lagos and the village to ensure we responded to all the letters.

The response to my calling for help came from young people from all over the world. My friends did not have the same interest in writing to pen pals, so they wrote once or twice and stopped. I continued to exchange letters with several of the pen pals, including one Miss Funke, who wrote from her secondary School at Yaba, Lagos. Some of my pen pals from the UK and Ireland stayed in contact for many years and during my first few years as a university student in the U.S.

I learned along the way that I would have to be conscious of calling out for help too often, but I also became aware that city life is impersonal. In the city, one has to make do alone; city life was unlike the village, where help was readily available even before one asked for it. The expression on one's face in the village was sufficient to draw the attention people who wanted to make sure one was okay. The city was a different ball game where help was not shared.

That hard lesson was not clear until my first trip to Lagos. I went alone. I travelled with a *kabukabu* driver—i.e., one who used unsavory ways and means to make money—who picked me up from Uselu along the Benin/Lagos road and dropped me off at the outskirts of the city in the area of Ikorodu Express Road.

Even for the person who has lived in Lagos, it was an awful challenge to get to Obalende, which was my final destination. There were no taxis at the place I was dropped off on the side of the eight-lane express highway. Of course, little did I know then that I could not afford to pay for the taxi anyway. I did not have much time to waste, since it was evening and would be getting dark shortly.

"What is the way to Obalende?" I tried to stop someone to ask them, but no one seemed to be willing to stop and listen. Changing my tactic, I started calling, "Sir! Please, sir, can you show me the direction to Obalende?"

The few who responded informed me I had not arrived in Lagos yet. "Mak yu tak the bus; folo am go to Eko."

I understood that to mean I must travel by bus going toward Lagos. Everyone was referring to the place I was going as Eko. It dawned on me then what a terrible mistake it had been to use the kabukabu on my first trip to Lagos.

I had never seen anything like this before. There was an endless chain of buses, called *molue,* which had originally been designed as tractor trailers but had been converted for use as public transporters.

The buses were loaded to maximum capacity and people were packed in tightly. No one seemed to care.

Everyone everywhere seemed to be in a mad rush to nowhere. Everyone seemed to have a busy mission which prevented them from talking to anyone. I felt like a disturbing nuisance interfering with the chaos of the moment. As the bus I picked left the place on the Ikorodu Express Road, I asked the *Agbero,* the young man who served as conductor, "Sir, where can I get off the bus? I am going to Obalende."

No one seemed to pay attention, but I kept asking where I should exit the bus. We must have gone by several bus terminals; I recall Yaba-Anthony and Ebute Meta. The conductors were yelling wildly but no one seemed to care. At one bus stop, I got off the bus and called for a taxi for help again, which did not draw any attention. I was crazy!

I have almost run out of money and was quite concerned about making the right decisions that would get me to Obalende. Eventually, someone pointed out a bus, but the conductor was yelling "Eko, Eko!"

In order to reassure myself that I was still travelling in the right direction, I asked, "Conductor, is the bus going to Obalende?" There was no response, but about halfway through the ride, he started shouting for Obalende. I started silently praying that it would take me to my destination. I was among the few passengers who left in the bus at the last stop. I got off the bus, frantically asking for Obalende.

A young man who had been on the same bus with me pointed to a street. "Walk and follow the directions to that street." I did exactly as was told and saw the street sign.

It was dark when I walked into the store where Philip was sewing clothes on the machine. *"Dabi kha-sor,"* said Philip. Which, in our dialect, was our way of saying, "I hope all is well at home. How is Mama and Baba?"

"Everyone is doing fine" I assured Philip.

Philip introduced me to one of his co-apprentices, showing off how proud he was at the moment. "Here is my younger brother."

"Ahaa, Philip, I didn't know you have a younger brother!" the apprentice said.

Afterwards, upon the assurances that nothing awful had happened at home and everyone was fine, Philip went on to inquire as to what brought me to Lagos. Philip knew from that moment on he was responsible for me. We tried to talk and make plans. There really was not much that could be accomplished that evening as darkness engulfed the noisy place. The city lights shone from the light poles and swarms of insects flew around the lights. Occasionally, someone carrying their wares on their head walked by as they returned home. I realized in was in a precarious, sobering situation. Philip was sharing the parlor/store with four other male apprentices. There was only one shower, shared by all the tenants. The toilet was a primitive latrine mounted on a platform, and the waste was collected underneath in a bucket.

With the constant smell of the dirty drainage in the gutters, the whole place had an air of decay. Not to mention the mosquitoes biting throughout the night. Realizing that I could have been sleeping on the street that impetuous night, I was resigned to be very thankful.

I spent the night sleeping on the floor, which was shared by all six of us. At dawn the next day, life resumed as normal for the city dwellers, but I was having profound thoughts about my survival and where I would go from there. That impromptu trip to live in Lagos was one of my last stunts.

We have an older brother, Albert Umoru Akhamie. He is the one Philip came to stay with during his first venture to Lagos on his own. "I can assure you that Umoru's place is worse off," Philip said. As a result, we ruled him out of our plan.

"No need to be seeking his help now. You know he has many

children, so we do not want to trouble him at all," I agreed.

Later on, Philip admitted, "Umoru was within walking distance."

"So why couldn't I see him" I asked Philip, trying to pressure him since Umoru was my favorite brother in those days.

"You are in Lagos and people here do not see each other like that. Everyone is busy around here. I have not seen him for quite a long time myself."

My heart sank a little bit, but given my situation and what I had experienced so far, I could not disagree with Philip. Also, I could not see any signs for optimism.

"After trying so much and gaining nothing; would it be unreasonable to return home in distress? I did not say out loud what I was thinking. I did not want to put too much pressure on Philip but rather allow him to figure things out for himself.

Later in the day Philip came up with an ambitious plan, which to a large extent resulted in the biggest impacts to my changing life. "You can go over and stay with Cobani," Philip told me.

"You mean Columbanus Etu is in Lagos?" I asked.

"Yes, he has been living in Lagos for a long time. I went to visit him at his place. It is very far from here."

"Oh yes!" one of the co-apprentices agreed. "It took him took most of a day to go there."

Columbanus is the firstborn of our sister Anima Akhamie, who is married to Luke Etu. He left a long time ago, before the Biafra War. He had a high rank in the military after the war, because his bodyguard, called *akolofos*, always accompanied him when he visited the village. He was a single man then, tall and very handsome. I made sure that I went to see him every time he came home to visit.

Philip decided it was not wise for me to venture out on my own to a new part of the Lagos metropolis called Festac Town. "I have a friend called Mike. He will take you in the evening after work to Columbanus' place in Festac."

"After work! You said it took you all day to go there," I reminded Philip.

"Do not worry," Philip and his co-workers assured me.

"Mike knows Lagos like the palm of his hand. He will be glad to do us a favor."

"Who is this man who has so much earned the trust of Philip?" I wondered and waited patiently. Like clockwork, Michael (Mike) Omesah came as Philip predicted. Mike lived in the Orile-Iganmu area and was obliged to take me there since going to Columbanus' was an extra trip from his place.

"Don't worry," Mike said with a smile. "We gonna go. Philipoh, see yah later."

I grabbed my bag and headed out with Mike.

I cannot recall what we talked about on the way, but I know I was still afraid of the commotion of hopping onto the noisy molues. But I was determined to keep up with Mike. Believe it or not, I came to understand later that Mike and I attended the same secondary school, Our Lady of Fatima.

Setting eyes on Festac Town was an attitude changer, even for a pessimistic downtrodden person. In contrast to the gloom and decay of Eko, Obalende, Ebute Meta, and other parts of Lagos I had seen on the way, Festac Town represented Nigeria with pride and promise. Suddenly, it seemed as if I had arrived in a modern city such as I had seen in the magazines. The streets were paved and marked with walkways for pedestals. Instead of dwelling on those past experiences, I accepted them as tests of willpower. To top it all, I was united with my oldest nephew. Columbanus (Banus) Etu, as my first nephew, held a place of special honor as Baba's oldest male grandchild. However, since I was the youngest of his uncles, out of respect I called him "brother." The same applied for my older nephews, brothers John Osikhemekhai and Tom Uloko.

Brother Banus was a calm man of dignity and did not say much, like his father and grandfather (my father). He had risen to the esteemed position of officer in the Nigerian Army. Although he left home as a teenager when I was very young, before the Biafra War, he knew me. Without any hesitation, he welcomed us in. "Brother mo! Eh eh! How is Baba," he inquired.

"Everyone was doing well at home," I assured him.

It was a comfortable place; I had the one bedroom to myself. Decent meals filled my hungry stomach for the rest of the time and kept my spirits high. I spent about three weeks at Banus' place in Festac Town, returning to the village for Christmas.

Chapter 20

The Welcoming Place

I enjoyed the comfort of village life, but there was nothing to excite me in the mundane things I had known all my life. At Benin City there was really no place where I could stay to while I figured out what I wanted to do. However, I liked the peacefulness of Festac Town in Lagos, and the more so when many of my mates who had not previously left Afowa amassed there to look for jobs in the city.

"One has to take advantage of the opportunities that are available. One should always take time to look within and around because opportunities in life are limitless." Such were the discussions with my colleagues, Tony, Jerome, and others. It became clearer to each one of us that we needed to find a way out.

We knew schooling in Nigeria had continued to evolve from the colonial era of standard schools in the 1950s and '60s to the secondary or grammar schools and colleges of the 1970s, and more, unlimited changes beyond. However, there was no consistent tracking, like that in the grade school system—i.e., first to fifth grades of elementary school; sixth to eighth grades of middle school; and ninth to twelve grades of high schools. Nigeria had created so many systems for teachers, commerce, technical, apprenticeships, and other professions. The one central theme was the completion of twelve years of schooling was considered as the basic standard for an educated person.

"You are on your own," were the words of advice for the majority of my mates when they graduated from high school. From that time onward you were expected to help yourself and take over some of the responsibilities of the family.

My fortune was the same thing that had handicapped me as "the lastborn." Aside from the goodness of my heart, I did not owe anyone much responsibility, which made it easy to focus on my life. My pathway was to pursue further education, which brought me as a teenager to the United States in 1981.

I went on to enroll at Eastern Washington University (EWU) in Cheney, Washington. With the designation of "foreign student," my Duration of Status (DS for short) allowed me to stay in the U.S. as long as I maintained a bona fide, fulltime student status, as well as the student F-1 visa status.

Help meeting those conditions was one of the fortunate aspects of EWU. They had a well-organized program, implemented under auspices of Professor Wong, the international students' advisor—i.e., professor, ombudsman, or guardian. Professor Wong handled immigration matters and served as the iron-clad guardian of the welfare of the international students.

Until my encounter with the Immigration and Naturalization Service (INS) later in that first year determined the trajectory of my life, I must admit life had worked well in my favor, although I was naïve about the burden of being a foreign student and about staying within the rules of law.

As an immigrant settling down for the beginning of an academic undertaking, I took many things for granted. Like the rookie or a parent taken for granted, Dr. Wong was to some extent disrespected by his international students. However, dedication to his position as the international students' advisor—especially in the first year—was essential for our success.

I stayed on campus, which was an excellent idea in regards to the comforts of daily living. I was able to focus on schooling without major distractions. Aside from the passing of my father, which was communicated through a letter that reached me a month after of his death, my focus was mainly on academics. Towards the end of the school year, in the spring of 1982, I had become worried about the matter of how I would continue my studies as a self-sponsored student. My student financial account was quickly running out.

Nowadays, I can reflect, based on my perspective of working at the Department of Homeland Security in a career of public service, that my coming to America was the ultimate venture. As such I am always mindful of how encounters have long-lasting impacts. Seemingly a huge nation of immigrants, I believed everyone could make it and things would work out well for everyone: After my enlistment in the U.S. Army, I was employed as INS Immigration Inspector in 1992; since then, due to rapid promotions; I went on to work in different career positions within the INS including; the director of Public Affairs; Asylum and Refugee officer; Examination and district adjudications officer, Special Agent, and Detention and Removal Officer. INS became DHS after the 9/11 terrorist attacks and I played the major role of Joint Terrorism Taskforce (JTTF) in working with the multitude of federal, states and local law enforcement agencies at the forefront of counterterrorism investigations.

For new arrivals, worry about the hype surrounding the politics of immigration should be avoided so as to not lower the yearning to succeed. Once one buys into the negative hype, the spirit of inferiority regarding one's home country sets in to weaken ambition. The African immigrants must rise mightily and never succumb to the idea that witchcraft, voodoo, or evil spirits have been sent to make life difficult. I have a pragmatic opinion, held by vast number of Americans, that, "Everyone, with the exception of the Native Americans and the slaves, came to the U.S. as an immigrant." I believe that the debate over immigration will continue into the future, well after those of us debating it now are gone.

However, for those of us not born in the U.S. but who have lived in it, we uphold the Constitution's guarantee of liberty for all. Just like the forgotten songs of my village that express, "The world that I told God I was going to, do not let it get in the way; do not let me fall so the enemy can laugh at me," we all must sing in the spirit of America, God bless thee.

There were no sources of employment in the university town of Cheney, Washington, or surrounding areas. I could not make enough to sustain myself and provide the funds for my college tuition. Besides, I would have had to receive work authorization and a social security card before venturing out to find a job. The odds were not in my favor at all. Such are the constraints and unanticipated aspects faced by immigrants coming to America.

Whether immigrant or foreign student, these situations of residing in the U.S. could flip over into burdens once the slightest mistake trips up even the well-intentioned person, which is what happened to me.

Foreign students pay higher tuition fees and are ineligible for any financial support, not even bank loans. After considering my available options, I decided that I would have to transfer to another university. I sought out places where jobs were plentiful and where I would be able to find a job. I applied to universities in the Midwest and received admission with the accompanying form I-20 from schools in Kansas and Oklahoma. Once I was assured of admission, I traveled back to Nigeria for the main purpose of transferring money for the second year. I also decided that I would venture out on my own as a way to find my niche.

Although my student visa was still in force under the DS, I returned to the embassy in Lagos and received an updated visa, using the form I-20 issued by Eastern Washington University. I did not inform anyone of my plan to transfer to another school. The mistake of naivety was set in motion, since I decided *not* to enroll at EWU but rather continue with my transfer plans to Oklahoma State University. The mistakes compounded rapidly, since the wire transfer went to EWU—based on the form I-20—for financial expenses for the academic school year 1982/83.

Allow me to re-introduce my situation of *wahala,* a Nigerian word for trouble! On returning to the U.S., I cleared Immigration and

Customs at John F. Kennedy International Airport in New York early in the morning. I was scheduled to depart from there to Spokane, Washington, but the wahala seemed to have opened like a torrent of water from a faucet when I informed the ticketing agent of my changed itinerary.

"There are no flights from here. You have to go to La Guardia Airport for domestic lights."

I repeated the name "La Guardia Airport," which showed I did not have a clue what had been said.

The ticket agent repeated, "You have to take the local transport. I recommend using the taxi so you don't get lost. At the other airport, the agent will help you."

Although I was able to change my trip to Oklahoma City; from where I would travel by greyhound bus to Oklahoma State University in Stillwater, the damage was done. Those self-inflicted problems came with the vulnerabilities of venturing into unknown territory. Without a travel companion, I left one of my suitcases behind when I exited the taxi at the terminal. It turned out to be a careless move to leave a bag and made it easy to steal. Scared from stories I had heard about New York and notorious taxi drivers stealing from foreigners, I continued on a downward spiral, one problem after the other.

I arrived at Oklahoma State University on the evening of that same day. Later, I went on to enroll for the fall semester, but the trouble with the INS loomed impatiently. While I was worried, I remained undaunted as I resumed full academic studies. I felt a tingle as to the severity of my mistakes when I contacted the international student advisor at Eastern Washington University to complete my transfer. OSU did not have an advisor like the one at EWU, so I did things without due diligence.

Although a highly recognized international institution, the office of the international students at Oklahoma State University was embedded within the office of admissions. There was no international student advisor to handle immigration and other cultural programs. The vacuum left many like me to fumble through overwhelming immigration matters.

The international student advisor at EWU revealed to me that my transfer was not approved by the INS since I did not receive prior authorization before enrolling in another university. In a letter from the INS, along with my cancelled visa, was the dreaded "Order of Deportation" which stated that I must depart from the United States within 30 days. The implications confirmed my ignorance.

"Dave, this is serious! You have to take it as a serious matter when the INS issues such an order of deportation," I was told.

Since no one had experienced such a problem before; I did not panic. I did not like OSU anyway because of the slow life, and I certainly did not want to continue in the same pattern of mistakes.

Before school was out for the winter semester, I contacted Lasarian, who I had known when growing up in Afowa and who was attending college in New Jersey. As I was explaining that I was calling from Oklahoma, he said out loud, "Oklaho - ma! What Oklahoma?" In the most sarcastic manner, he asked, "Is that in a village in the United States?"

Whether it was intended as a joke, his emphatic repeating of "Oklahoma" prompted me to disclose my situation. "I received a letter from the INS that I must depart from the U.S. because I transferred from my previous university without permission." I was careful not to complicate things by mentioning EWU in Washington State.

Lasarian's elder brother, who was an old boy from my high school at Our Lady of Fatima, overheard the conversation. At that very moment, Evaristus Oshiokpekhai—now a medical doctor—came on the phone and informed me that it was a serious matter that required immediate action on my part.

"You have to leave that place," Evaristus said. I later realized that the letter from INS was my bag and baggage letter (commonly known as "B and B"); which the "run" letter, in which case one must change locations in case they come looking for the illegal person.

By December of 1982, in the midst of my period of the "threshing floor"—as in the biblical reference—I packed my luggage. I left my car in the care of Silvanus Udoka—now a professor in North Carolina—and flew out of Oklahoma City to Newark Airport in New Jersey. Regrets about the conversations, encounters, and problems with the INS were turned into a beacon of hope when I met the dynamic personality of Evaristus Oshiokpekhai, who was an angelic one in the time of my threshing floor.

"It has been two years since I left Nigeria. I must admit that I feel like I have arrived in the U.S. for the first time."

"David-David, what are you talking about?" Evaristus asked as we drove in his older brother Thomas Oshiokpekhai's Oldsmobile Cutlass Supreme around Newark and New York.

"Well, you see, I have never seen so many black people. When we used to see a black person, we waved and said hello."

"Here is like Lagos. Everyone is relaxed and seems happy!"

Evaristus took me as his younger brother and friend to his school, which was called Kean College of New Jersey at the time, and I was enrolled as a non-matriculated student.

"Do not worry about all the formalities about the name of a university or college. Once you are enrolled in school and taking more than twelve credit hours, the INS will not bother with you."

Another student called Albert was in a similar predicament involving changing schools, and he had no money, so he decided to return to Nigeria and reapply for admission after he had resolved the situation. Albert was not able to return to the United States once he left.

It should be understood that a bump on the road does not mean one must give up. Rather, one must look around so as not to be the first to quit just because people said no. There are countless stories to tell about my activities as a student at Kean College, where I found myself among laudable folks who took personal interest to nurture me. Kean College said, "Yes," and set me on my pathway, which is what makes it crucial to recount the remarkable people like Mr. Audley Bridges, a descendent of generations of slaves, and Professor Peggy Dunn, a white woman who became my adopted mother.

Mr. Bridges seized upon the high-mindedness of establishing an office of international students within the admissions office as he welcomed us (the "foreign born idiots"), making the college an auspicious oasis. As such he epitomized the African proverb of, "*Ai gbierere*," which in Afemai dialect means, "We do not kill visitors, but welcome them." Mr. Bridges welcomed many students such as me, thereby paving the way for many to take courses, even when they could not pay the tuition fees at the time of registration. As in my case, I owe a debt of gratitude to the one who stood by me when others shunned me.

"How come you're not going to school? Classes are starting next week, you know."

"Yes, I know, but I do not have the money to pay at in-person registration. I still owe from last semester."

"That does that mean you cannot go to school for the whole semester. You don't have to pay before you register. Why don't you just use another name?"

He was right. The more I thought about that exchange with a fellow student—a Yoruba man—the more confident I became. I went over to the college for the afternoon in-person registration and registered for six courses, a total of eighteen credit hours.

One or two students at the front of the line were called over to discuss payment of past due fees. Instead of taking my turn to explain my situation, I switched lines and moved over to the lines for students who had been cleared. It was printed in bold letters: ACCOUNT CLEARANCE.

"Here is my registration form." I was a little bit nervous in front of the accounting staff; however, I was being attended to by a white student who did not know the African names from A to Z. He marked the form as cleared. I spelled my last name, skipping the first letter and starting with Z, and then changed it back to A after I cleared accounting. I had already sent a request for my brother Peter to transfer the money to pay my tuition, which arrived before the commencement period, so I cleared the balance I owed.

Not showing my face at the business office was my way of avoiding getting caught, even when I was invited to discuss my excellent academic performance of making the dean's list. Sneaking in and through the lines during in-person registration worked out in my favor. I completed the requirements for a baccalaureate degree, but I did not know I was listed for graduation in May of 1985, since I had completed the course requirements by December 1984. It was astounding, entering the U.S. in 1981 and graduating Cum Laude within three years.

Dr. Peggy Dunn was the first to encourage my writing and so awaken my knack of storytelling. She held me by the hand as a mother through the doubts. As a professor, she was one of the best, but I learned that I have something to contribute to society; even if it is as small a gesture as coming to class, interacting, and discussing African folklore.

She would say in the oral interpretation class, "Focus on your strength, make it work, because the things you know come to you always. You can always improve on your style, and you will do great things."

Every student received personal attention; and everyone appreciated her as our real coach. We had an ordained minister as a classmate who was encouraged to rely on the skills of giving sermons, and he went on to complete the program as a better preacher.

During one of my last conversations as an alumni, I posed one of those inquisitive questions as I had done with my mother. "Since I have noticed that you have never discussed your family in class, I wanted to find out if you have children."

Without giving much it much thought, she said, "You are my children, you and your classmates!"

Her words turned me around in a full circle because the professor had a better understanding of my need to be close to my mother than I realized. Later on, as many years have passed, I have memories of her words, and as I travel throughout the U.S. during my career at DHS, I have hoped that I would come in contact with Dr. Dunn or her family members. I am happy to call her my mother.

At times, the perception might have been that foreign students were seen as roaming from one college or university to another. But wherever we went, we had two particular things in common. We had hope for a better life and attaining the dream that was imbedded in the titles of MD, PhD, MBA, and JD. We worked hard, and like many of our fellow students, we have achieved great things. Some who thought they could not afford the school fees left school and went on different paths. But most of us stuck to it and as such affirmed that in America, someone like me, who was slated for deportation, could attain military experience, a professional career in public service, and educational achievement such as my Juris Doctorate in Law.

Chapter 21

Beyond the Ripples of Desert Storm

Not long after I obtained a Bachelor's Degree in English/Speech/Theatre/Media, I decided to join the military. I had been working on a Master's in Public Administration at my alma mater on a graduate assistant scholarship, but I was not doing well and left after the first year. After I left, I couldn't believe that I had walked away from the tuition-free master's program. But I reflected on my personal character to do things and to seek out other opportunities and asked myself, "What shall I do next?"

My colleagues in similar situations went to the military recruiters. One joined and was shipped to boot camp for army basic training around Christmas of 1987. The idea of what I should do next was unsettled, so in January of 1988, I drove over to the recruiting station on Stuyvesant Avenue in Union, NJ, to inquire about military service. I had heard that the military would pay for one's training, take care of the man's family, and pay for housing. I met a black woman in military uniform (Staff Sergeant Battle) as I walked into the office. She provided information regarding how to join the Army. After a brief conversation, she insisted that I take a practice test. "You have to pass the test before you can qualify to join the Army," Sgt. Battle said.

I took the assessment test and I passed. Thereafter, she typed up an agreement based on what had transpired—which I signed—and I volunteered to join the U.S. Army.

I returned home to tell my wife, Tiwana Akhamie, what had happened. She said, "I do not know what to say. I trust that you will do the right thing."

Some of my friends understood that I had to make a manly decision, but others thought it was a laughable matter that I had joined the U.S. Army.

"David, you cannot be serious about going in the military. What if you have to fight in a war?" My friends questioned my decision as I waited to go to basic training.

I tried to explain in the best way that I could. "I do not believe there is going to be war, so there is no matter of getting killed or killing other people. Besides, young people are getting killed on the streets everywhere. You are from Nigeria, so talk less. Remember the dead bodies that were left dead for days on the streets in Oshodi? I have already signed up, and if I do not go, they are going to mess me up. You know that!"

In 1990, barely two years into active duty, my unit was one of the first to be deployed from Germany to Kuwait. Our mission was to participate in the international coalition that would liberate Kuwait from occupation by Iraq. It was a mission to bring peace to the people of Kuwait, but it resulted in the First Gulf War against Iraq.

On December 7, 1990, we departed Stuttgart, Germany, to our destination in Kuwait. We landed at what is now Bahrain International Airport. Once we boarded the plane, my mind began to ponder the events in my life that had led to this moment, which actually marked the beginning of this story. I began to deliberate whether I was really going to a war. I found myself wondering whether war served as the ultimate solution to the world's problems.

Pathway to Promise

Private First Class Akhamiemona

In the midst of tense times of war, my thoughts were about my loved ones: my wife and two little girls I had left behind in Karlsruhe, Germany. Also, thoughts of my mother would suddenly come streaming into my consciousness. I wondered how my mother would fit into all the happenings in my life. I thought of my father, who had passed away after I left home. I was making the voyage to Kuwait, concerned about war and even more so about my future. Up until that moment, I had never really given any thought about fighting in a war. Whether I would live through the coming period of conflict, or what would happen in my life in the future, was unknown.

When I had enlisted, the decision whether or not to take another person's life in a war was my least concern. Now, as reality dawned, I recalled the wonderful days of my childhood. I simply allowed my subconscious mind to indulge in the remembered moments of peace.

Now and then, I looked back at those names Mama used to praise me. *"Adebidi, Asa-mali, Oghie luku-luku, Oghieneni, Odala-ubile,"* She used such names in the moments when she wanted me to go the extra mile and to do something beyond my current state or when she welcomed my presence. At times I could hear her voice ringing out the names, one after the other.

I would display charming smiles. I smiled a lot then and held such moments in high regard as building my character. Whenever she called these names, I felt good inside, filled with the spirit of love and courage. Such moments made the little boy in me become a man as the sparks ignited boldness of mind. The smiles were my way of showing love and respect in return.

One might question why it was important to make the little boy feel like he was a man. It was a matter of implanting a sense of responsibility. At times, Mum's praises could be extravagant, like when she wanted me to smile when I was moody. But I later realized that my mother was using her strategies to instill positive images and attitudes. I also realized that, like my mother, other people used such positive actions as to insure greatness and virtue in their own young sons.

With those childhood nicknames of praise, I found happiness in the way each person forms their own favorite versions of themselves. A good name can positively shape a child's character and mold the child in the shape of those people who originally bore their name. For the most part, my mother used my name to instill happy memories.

Growing up in a large household, everyone took notice of how calling me those nicknames made me smile. Other relatives around the household joined in addressing me with nicknames like Ogieneni. In the Uzairue dialect, the nickname Oghieneni means "the king," and it means the "the superior king of kings."

I recognize that there are several nuances of similarities between my name and the biblical King David. I was the lastborn, as was the case with King David, and another coincidence was the nicknames of Oghieneni and Oghie luku luku; both were praises for the king. I decided that I was well suited to be a David and found no irritation with being addressed as Ogieneni. For a brief moment I reflected on the coincidence that David, a last child, became an important person from the ripple effects of war and victory over Goliath.

My thoughts about childhood focused on my first memories of the sights and sounds of the village. The more vivid the image, the more it stuck to my mind. I was fond of wild, flowering plants, green vegetation, and fallen leaves. Nature was my fantasy, and I was fascinated by the picture of a blue sky's image reflected on the water's surface. My dislikes involved darkness and grooming.

In those days, it was tough to raise children, and boys were the toughest. I give thanks to and praise my mother, who had mastered the key to unlocking the complexities and stubborn inner self of my being. She had experience raising my older siblings before I was born. I was not her lastborn, but the last baby to survive, since the three after me were stillborn. I have heard stories of a mother's joy and the sorrowful experiences of infant mortality.

Whenever thoughts of my mother came to mind, I was conscious of those mighty names of courage she gave me that never ceased, even when I became a grown man.

As I returned to the consciousness of the present, in my seat on that plane on the way to Kuwait, I reflected on how Mother would encourage me, even in this present situation of war.

Chapter 22

My Diaspora

After my military service, time moved swiftly without any urge to repeat Mother's feat of planting her seeds of greatness. About the age of forty and thereafter, the moments of my childhood were rekindled. Some of my colleagues have experienced post-traumatic stress and other issues in their subconscious. Mine invoked dreams entangled by the agony of Mother's suffering and the transient moments which continued to linger. A year passed, and another similar situation would follow, and gradually my dreams became a series of occurrences, mostly in the same location of my village.

The first in the series of dreams was a brightening light that appeared like flares at Ugholomi. It bothered me, but it was only a short-lived feeling. Sometimes, the feeling was like a rush of shivers during nights in the desert or chills during a cold snap.

My diaspora involves the period my stay in the United States and the travels to my native home: I traveled to Nigeria in 2005. It was the first time since Mother passed and also the first time I was reunited with Philip. I was reunited with all of my siblings. For long, I had accepted the reality of being the baby brother, but Philip had strayed from the family for many years, almost two decades. After our mother passed in 1991, I had not had any contacts with him. I was at Peter's house in Port Harcourt when he received a call from Philip. "That was Philip," Peter said. "The line went dead before I could tell him that you were here."

"Philip! I did not know you were in contact with Philip. It would have been nice to speak with him." I said, to let Peter know I would have talked with Philip.

Pastor Peter A. Akhamie

Peter went on to explain how the childhood pattern of behaviors had remained with everyone. Philip was still unsettled and had avoided contact with everyone, even with our uncle Sunday and his family at Okpella.

Peter said, "Oh no, he just called me out of the blue. It has been a long time since I have heard from him."

"Philip is still with the woman from Okpella?"

"Yes. He has all sorts of problems because he was deceived into thinking he was going to make money through that woman."

"No man should have to depend on a woman."

Peter's wife, Priscilla, raised her eyes.

"I do not ask my wife to give me money. She would not let me forget," I said jokingly. "That Okpella woman has taken over Philip's life and uses him like her small boy!"

"It is terrible that Philip has let someone take over his life," Peter answered.

We agreed that such a thing happens when a man is enticed by a rich woman because he does not want to work hard on his own to raise a family.

At Afowa, in the early hours of morning, I requested that we go to find Philip. With my nephew and Priscilla, we drove to Auchi. Coincidentally, it was same week of the Uzairue market, and Philip had to spend the night with his friends at Auchi, from where he would go to the market. I brought along a video recorder.

Feelings of tension came over me the moment we saw Philip, his wife, and his grown, teenage stepson. I was uncertain what to do or whether I must do something to make the best of this moment.

The emotion was equally intense for everyone, but Priscilla calmed the situation. "Have a seat!" She said. She went over to Philip's wife and embraced her, after which everyone shared embraces.

So it is the young man who beats Philip, I thought, seeing the tall, adolescence male in the room. I could not come up with any words.

Philip and son Solomon

"This is my brother from overseas. David," Philip called out happily. In his own ways, Philip may have strayed from us, "but the blood within is the same," as in the saying that blood is thicker than water.

I called him aside. "Let's have a talk," I offered mindful advice to Philip. I told him that the blood in our veins would prove stronger than any outside forces.

Philip has always been free minded, but we knew how to take advantage of the moment and hide the emotional injuries from self-inflicted sorrows in life. I reminded Philip, "Do not play *wayo* on me." We both laughed about my hints on the thing we both knew quite well, which is the use of emotional displays. Money was hard to get from anyone, so Philip relied on trickeries to get money from Mama. But Mother was gone and I wouldn't let him suck me into talks about her.

"Philip, Mama is gone. She passed on at her time, just as all of us will do at our own times. We are getting old, so each of us must make the best of our lives."

"Ok, ok! What did you bring for me?" He smiled as if he were asking for money. Although I had already given his share of dollars to Peter to hold for him, I said, "I do not have any money. I have a family now. It is very expensive to raise children in the U.S. Money does not come easy like it does here. Every little thing costs money. No one gives money to anyone for free!" I said, trying to be sarcastic.

"You have many nephews and nieces all over the place, so you have to represent yourself as their uncle," Philip replied.

It was a tough act on my part, but the moment we were separated I felt that I loved him. Philip did not let me leave with empty hands. Before we said our goodbyes, he gave me a piece of cloth to take home. His gift showed the kind heart that allowed Philip to pave the way for me as a teenager that time when I went to meet him in Lagos. His kindness reaffirmed Mama's adage to "find the good side of everyone."

Philip has not changed his ways from the time we were kids when Mother taught him how to be disciplined. He has continued to live for the moment, like the one "whose hand wouldn't let do," which was Mama's saying to Philip when he was not determined and would not focus. Philip laughed, smiled, and was as happy as a player, which was how he got over on us to give him everything. Philip still believed that someone had to take care of him instead of him working hard to earn his own way.

Upon returning to my place in Woodbridge, Virginia, from the trip to Nigeria, my evocative dreams returned. However, they were clearer versions of that same water theme and the scenes of Ugholomi. A theme began to emerge of the revered characters which Mother had instilled in my childhood—that as a dreamer I must believe in my dreams.

Remembering the days of letters when it took a long time to communicate over long distances, I realized I could now talk on the phone with anyone anywhere in an instant. Over the telephone I recounted one my dreams about me and our mother at Ugholomi. By his deep pause, I could sense Peter was curious, which prompted me to ask, "Are you still there? Can you hear me? Do you think Mama was reaching out through my dreams?"

"No, that couldn't be our mother, because she is dead," Peter said. "A person should to be careful when dreams involve images of departed loved ones, because demons often try to mimic a departed loved one's image. Do not idolize manifestations of water spirits."

The dreams of Ugholomi, in my view, are permeated with superstition, and based on Peter's cautioning, I would have to tread carefully. I have heard stories of *mami wata* residing in the rivers and seas. Such stories of the existence of mami wata—mermaids—and other unknown entities of the water are commonplace in every culture. All of humanity is innately superstitious.

My quest to find the meaning of the dreams, with their interconnected creative forces, inspired ideas and rekindled the lure to write. As a child, the pond of clear-standing water and its shadow mimicking the blue sky intrigued me. For the most part, the more I thought of the vivid imagery, the more I saw the images of sky on water.

When I looked directly into the small pool of water, I saw the thrilling ripples of the panoramic image of the sky cast onto that small puddle on the ground. The ripples, the imagery of layers, and the blue sky merged together in that pond's mirror image. When I gazed at my reflection, feelings of imbalance invoked sensations like one falling into the sea. At times I actually stepped inside the pool of water, stirred it up a bit to assure my senses there was no danger.

I was enthralled by the thrill of ripples on water ponds. Out of curiosity or perhaps just for fun, I joined other kids to throw rocks and little pebbles to stir the pool into waves. We watched as the ripples spiraled away. Similar chilling sensations would come over me when I recalled the dreams. The situations they presented were either frightening fairytales or the superstitions which pervaded our lives during the years we were growing up in the village.

I recalled how my mother comported with me when I told her about the scary dreams. We talked and she would always provide reassurances. At times she would give calming words, such as, "You must go to church." When things had seemed hopeless, she said, "Call the name Jesus." It was how I came to the idea of calling, "Jesus," and I have relied on her advice.

Faith and superstition continue to be the mysteries of humanity. Some have claimed they know all about the nitty-gritty of humanity and taught us faith as say; "faith is a supernatural gift from God which enables us to believe without doubting whatever God has revealed." I have found for myself that people are less inclined to talk about the intricacies of their beliefs, which is the reason I relied on my mother.

Lacking an explanation for things unknown, such the water of Ugholomi coming from underground, people looked at the notion of mystical powers. I believed some of those superstitious stories which were circulated. There was such a story among the young people that claimed if one were easily tickled, it was a sign that bad things would happen, and the black insect's sting would cure the ticklishness.

The tiny, black-water insects were only found at Ugholomi. When I heard the story, I thought it was something that I would have to prove to myself. In the company of other kids, I placed one of the black insects under my armpit until it stung. Whether it worked did not matter, as I released the insect to swim away. What mattered was that Mother was quick to separate me from such superstitions and, instead, implant her faith in Christianity.

In December 2017, while working on this story, I traveled to Nigeria; landed in Lagos where I stayed with Peter at Lekki; which is one of the newest areas of Lagos State. Peter and Allen Zibiri (a native of Afowa) took me on the trip to Afowa. We agreed to spend three nights at Thomas Uloko's hotel-resort. On my insistence that I tour those places of my childhood that I frequented; Peter agreed that Allen should go with me. Peter said;

"The farm is not what you used to know. There is nothing there to remind you of the hut, cocoa farm and the mango trees." He continued, "The new road has changed everything. There is no longer the footpath to Ugholomi. They buy water from the tanker, so no one fetches water at Ugholomi. There is no way you will recognize the place."

Philip was not there to accompany on any of my trips which allowed me to cover grounds to Ivbie Imiakhebu and Okpella to see uncle Sunday and family. Without Philip I resorted to sharing the most part of my home visit with Peter. On the way to Okpella we saw the thriving business of rock quarry located in the expanse of land between Uzairue and Okpella clans. We stopped at the University of Edo, located at Iyamho-Uzairue. The change all over Uzairue was evident that things have improved life for the better. Peter explained that the business was going to be profitable for many years to come.

Peter, Moses Abu and I posed with uncle Sunday and his family during my visit in December 2017

Afowa ; the special tree with the fruit hanging by strings

As I walked through the village I noticed that plants and trees have shown the sign of hope which eluded the people. I talked to my family members about the abundance of resources I found everywhere. The trees (some medicinal) have continued to blossom where they were not planted. I found palm trees, cashew tress, and Moringa – Miracle tree flourishing and some of the trees were cut-down to prevent overgrowths.

I saw my own diaspora has undergone a full circle of hopeless despair to hope; Philip came to me and Peter at the Thomas Uloko resort. It was time of dinner and Peter called the staff to order our meals I ordered the semolina and egusi soup. Philip looked as if was beaten and somewhat emaciated as if he lost weight. Peter asked him:

"Philip, what is wrong with you; you look so thin!" Philip raised and lifted his shirt showing his stomach. I said;

"He lost weight, is it not a good thing?" Philip interjected; as he showed his stomach

"I am hungry. Sometimes, I don't eat, but once in a whole day. I do not have the food to eat."

I caught sight of Peter's expression of tempered frustrations. He told Philip;

"If you cannot feed yourself now at your age what are you going to doing when you are over sixty?" Philip thought for a while and said. "Em; I will be Ok. I will do fine."

The dinner was severed so I gave half of my dish to Philip who was still eating pounded yam and egusi. The expression of despair never left his face throughout the time we spent at the village. The next day, Philip came back to see me since I asked him to bring me a good picture of himself. It was during our impromptu conversation with Paul, Anthony Philip, and I; that the situation of despair afflicting everyone came to the forefront: My father's big house that inspired many when I was a child was dilapidated. Both Paul and Peter have retired and were the elders of Akhamie's family.

Our parent's gravesites were next to each other side by side and appeared in deplorable condition to my dislike that made me very uncomfortable. I felt there was too much neglect and apathy that I should stay away from visiting the village. However, Philip was still in his own ways of asking for money; worst of all, it seemed to have spread throughout the village. Almost all the young men of my age and younger adults were out there asking for money. One lady was bold enough to ask me for settle; which was the Nigerian desperate ways of taking money under duress. My nephews we grew up together hassled as I wanted to say goodbye.

In my disgust, I complained to Peter the behavior people constantly expecting one to give money and I was resigned to extent that I will not want to return back to our home. I said, "There was no orderliness like when we grew up. The new road divided the village into half; no one walked anymore for a stroll." I resorted to hopping on the motorcycle taxi like everyone to move around and return to the guesthouse.

On a day that everyone was to be gone to the farm or work, the men at the village sat around waiting for palm wine to be brought to them. I knew many of the people who were younger when I was living at home. It seemed no one had any shame anymore and asking one to give them money. The village square was no longer there. The men and their age groups were not guarding the village.

I came to a conclusion that in my diaspora, my message is unambiguously clearer that there was an abundance of land for anyone who wished to take advantage of the natural resources. It was an affirmation that I would take a stand so that no one could force me to leave my native home.

Everyone follows the pathways of life. It is a matter of whether one allows fear of the unknown to derail them, and if they then capitulate on their purpose for living. I have witnessed for myself the multitude of excuses for things I detested, which I feared so much along Afowa's footpaths; from Izobo of idol sacrifices, ghosts and onto the cemetery for dead babies. Now they no longer exist. What has remained involves the purposes of living; my dreams which have been rekindled from the dreams of my mother. The dreams reaffirm that one faces the slippery rough scorched-earth roads to go far beyond; and no one can scare us away from the Pathway to Promise.

www.ingramcontent.com/pod-product-compliance
Lightning Source LLC
Chambersburg PA
CBHW071901290426
44110CB00013B/1236